# Overcoming Sinful Thoughts

Other books by Rev. T. G. Morrow
from Sophia Institute Press

*Overcoming Sinful Anger*
*How to Master Your Emotions and Bring Peace to Your Life*

*Christian Dating in a Godless World*

Rev. T.G. Morrow

# Overcoming Sinful Thoughts
## How to Realign Your Thinking and Defeat Harmful Ideas

SOPHIA INSTITUTE PRESS
Manchester, New Hampshire

*This book is dedicated
to God's most wonderful thought,
our Blessed Mother, Mary.*

# Contents

# Introduction

What is a sinful thought? A wrong thought. Well, it's more than that. It's a wrong thought that makes a difference in your spiritual journey. Thinking that America was discovered in 1498 is a wrong thought, but it is not likely to affect your chances of being saved. Or thinking that Alexander the Great never existed is wrong, but it isn't likely to hurt your chances to make it to the kingdom.

On the other hand, thinking that there is no hell, or that we deserve everything we have, or that we need not be concerned about venial sins could very well hamper our spiritual progress. These are the sorts of sinful thoughts we will be considering.

Thomas Aquinas wrote that there may be sin in the reason "if it errs in the knowledge of truth." So a sinful thought is a wrongheaded religiously significant thought, especially when one is in error "about what he is able and ought to know."[1] Is it then sinful to embrace a thought that one is not able to know is wrong? Although that is not a sin against God, it is what we call a material sin. That is, it is something that is wrong, but the person who embraces the thought is invincibly (blamelessly)

---

[1] St. Thomas Aquinas, *Summa Theologiae*, I-II, q. 74, art. 5.

ignorant. A material sin causes harm even though it does not willfully go against God.

For example, "I will do anything to avoid loneliness" or "Going to confession is too embarrassing" or "I'm just aiming for purgatory" might not be thoughts that everyone knows are wrong. Whereas thoughts such as "I don't have to help the poor" or "I don't have to love my enemies" should be clearly wrong to anyone who has read or heard Sacred Scripture. Nonetheless, all these thoughts are harmful whether we know it or not.

The purpose of this work is to identify some of the more common (and some not so common) erroneous thoughts that hold us back from developing intimacy with God. And, using biblical and philosophical arguments, I will attempt to explain why they are wrong. My assumption is that those reading this book will accept such arguments, if well made, and will change their wrong thoughts to embrace the truth and that those who already realize that these thoughts are wrong will be better equipped to explain why the thoughts are wrong to their acquaintances who may bring them up. For example, the questioning of God's existence in light of the world's suffering is a frequent argument of atheists. Extra attention will be given to that argument. And the idea that heaven will be boring is sometimes held by the young.

So, I will attempt to point out the error of sinful thoughts and to replace them with the truth. The truth will set us free.

1

# "I Am the Best"

*All those who are arrogant are an abomination to the LORD;*
*be assured, they will not go unpunished.*

— Proverbs 16:5

Once, on the feast of St. Lawrence, the Lord showed St. Margaret of Cortona an indescribably magnificent throne in heaven. On it she saw St. Francis of Assisi sitting. The Lord said to her, "Tell your Fathers, the Friars Minor, that the splendid throne which you saw among the angels was that of Lucifer.... My elect, Francis, is seated there today in resplendent glory." The Lord told her that Lucifer had lost his place by his sinful pride. It was given to Francis for his great humility.[2]

St. Francis built his Franciscan order on humility and poverty. His friars were to seek the last place in all things and thus were named the Order of Friars Minor. The founder's extraordinary humility was displayed on many occasions, not least of which the one captured in the following story.

[2] Most Rev. Ange-Marie Hiral, OFM, *The Revelations of Margaret of Cortona*, trans. Raphael Brown (N.p.: Franciscan Institute, 1952).

3

Once when Saint Francis was returning from the forest and from prayer, being on the way out of the forest, the one called Friar Masseo wanted to test how humble he was, and encountering him he said almost provocatively: "Why to you, why to you, why to you?" Saint Francis answered: "What is it that you want to say?" Friar Masseo said: "I say why does the whole world follow you, and every person seems to want to see you, to hear you, and to obey you? You are not a good looking man in body, you are not of great learning, you are not noble, why then does everyone want to follow you?" Hearing this, Saint Francis, altogether overjoyed in spirit ... turned to Friar Masseo and said: "Do you want to know why me? Do you want to know why me? Do you want to know why the whole world follows me? This I learned that the most holy eyes of God did not see among sinners any one more vile, more insufficient, or a greater sinner than me.[3]

## The Saints on Humility

Other great saints also stressed the importance of this virtue. "Once I was pondering why our Lord was so fond of this virtue of humility," wrote St. Teresa of Ávila, "and this thought came to me — in my opinion not as a result of reflection but suddenly: It is because God is supreme Truth; and to be humble is to walk in truth, for it is a very deep truth that of ourselves we have nothing good but

---

[3]  *The Little Flowers of St. Francis*, as quoted in "Father Canta-lamessa on Francis of Assisi's Humility," ZENIT, December 13, 2013, https://www.ewtn.com/catholicism/library/father-cantalamessa-on-francis-of-assisis-humility-5962.

only misery and nothingness."[4] Another Doctor of the Church, St. Catherine of Siena, reported God's words this way: "Do you know, daughter, who you are and who I am? If you know these two things you will have beatitude within your grasp. You are she who is not, and I AM HE WHO IS."[5] This was God's way of reminding her of the essence of humility—namely, that before God we are nothing. This brings to mind the "nada" doctrine of St. John of the Cross:

> To reach satisfaction in everything, desire
> satisfaction in nothing.
> To come to possession of everything, desire
> the possession of nothing.
> To arrive at being all, desire to be nothing.
> To come to the knowledge of everything,
> desire the knowledge of nothing.[6]

On another occasion, the Lord told St. Catherine of Siena, "[One] proves his humility on a proud man, his faith on an infidel, his true hope on one who despairs, his justice on the unjust, his kindness on the cruel, his gentleness and benignity on the irascible."[7] In other words, if you can be humble with a proud

4   St. Teresa of Ávila, *The Interior Castle*, in *The Collected Works of St. Teresa of Ávila*, vol. 2, trans. Kieran Kavanaugh and Otilio Rodríguez (Washington, DC: Institute of Carmelite Studies, 1980), 420.

5   Raymond of Capua, *Life of Catherine of Siena* (Rockford, IL: TAN Books, 2009), 92.

6   St. John of the Cross, *Ascent of Mount Carmel*, in *The Collected Works of St. John of the Cross*, trans. Kieran Kavanaugh, OCD, and Otilio Rodríguez, OCD (Washington, DC: Institute of Carmelite Studies, 1979), bk. 1, chap. 13.

7   *Dialogue of St. Catherine of Siena*, trans. Algar Thorold (N.p.: Cosimo, Incorporated, 2007), 48.

person, you are truly humble. St. Francis de Sales had something similar to say: "If, when stung by slander or ill-nature, we wax proud and swell with anger, it is a proof that our gentleness and humility are unreal, and mere artificial show."[8]

Of course, Jesus had much to say about pride and humility. For example, "The greatest among you will be your servant. All who exalt themselves will be humbled, and all who humble themselves will be exalted" (Matt. 23:11–12). The Magnificat of Mary is a classic example of humility praised and pride denounced:

> He has shown strength with his arm;
> he has scattered the proud in the thoughts of
> their hearts.
> He has brought down the powerful from their thrones,
> and lifted up the lowly. (Luke 1:51–52)

*Pride* is mentioned 138 times in one way or another in Sacred Scripture — nearly always as something to be avoided, as in Proverbs 16:5 at the head of this chapter. *Humility, humble*, and similar words appear 106 times, always as something to strive for.

One need not be a Christian to recognize the virtue of humility. Gandhi wrote that humility is an indispensable virtue to find the truth: "The seeker after truth should be humbler than the dust. The world crushes the dust under its feet, but the seeker after truth should so humble himself that even the dust could crush him."[9]

One need not even be religious to understand that pride is a vice. Just observe how we are repulsed by an athlete or a politician

---

[8] St. Francis de Sales, *Introduction to the Devout Life* (N.p.: Devoted Publishing, 2017), 77.

[9] Mohandas Gandhi, *An Autobiography: The Story of My Experiments with Truth*, trans. Mahadev Desai (Boston: Beacon Press, 1993), 7.

who is always proclaiming how wonderful he or she is. Anyone who has ever sought a loving relationship should know that one must place oneself beneath the beloved to achieve oneness. We offer our love and hope it will be returned.

It should be noted that pride can be good in one sense, as in a person taking pride in his work or a mother taking pride in her daughter. It can be legitimate satisfaction or pleasure about doing something well or the accomplishment of a friend or family member. When you say of your daughter who has done something good, "I'm proud of you," it is not the sin of pride but the virtue of encouragement. When you say, "I take pride in serving my customers," that is not sinful pride but satisfaction in doing something good for others. And as St. John Henry Newman taught, Christians should want to serve: "It is the Christian's excellence to be ... willing to serve, and to rejoice in permission to do so; to be content to view himself in a subordinate place; to love to sit in the dust."[10]

St. Francis of Assisi spoke of the humility of God: "O sublime humility! O humble sublimity! The Lord of the universe, God and the Son of God, so humbles himself that for our salvation He hides himself, under an ordinary piece of bread! Brothers, look at the humility of God and pour out your hearts before Him."[11] And, of course, in order to save us, Jesus took the "form of a slave":

[10] John Henry Newman, *The Heart of Newman: A Synthesis*, arranged by Erich Przywara (San Francisco: Ignatius Press, 1997), 278.

[11] St. Francis of Assisi, *Letter to the Entire Order*, in *Francis of Assisi: The Saint*, ed. Regis J. Armstrong, OFM Cap.; J. A. Wayne Hellman, OFM Conv.; and William J. Short, OFM (New York: New City, 1999), 118.

Though he was in the form of God,
  [Jesus] did not regard equality with God
  as something to be exploited,
but emptied himself,
  taking the form of a slave,
  being born in human likeness.
And being found in human form,
  he humbled himself
  and became obedient to the point of death —
  even death on a cross. (Phil. 2:6–8)

The saints took the example of Christ to heart. St. John of the Cross wrote that "all the visions, revelations and feelings from heaven, or whatever else one may desire to think upon, are not worth as much as the least act of humility."[12] Another St. John, John Vianney, taught, "Humility is to the various virtues what the chain is to a rosary. Take away the chain and the beads are scattered; remove humility and all virtues vanish." Maria Faustina, the Divine Mercy saint, wrote, "O Jesus, when I am in the last place, lower than the postulants, even the youngest of them, then I feel that I am in my proper place. I did not know that the Lord had put so much happiness in these drab little corners."[13]

No one valued humility more highly than St. Francis de Sales, who claimed that it "drives away Satan and keeps the graces and gifts of the Holy Spirit safe within us." Yet he found that it is a very elusive virtue. You may pray and pray for humility, and strive to live this virtue, and finally say, "At last I am humble"—and

[12] *Ascent of Mount Carmel*, 227.
[13] *Divine Mercy in My Soul: Diary of Saint Maria Faustina Kowalska* (Stockbridge, MA: Congregation of Marians of the Immaculate Conception, 1987), 106.

then you have lost it. Francis wrote, "Professions of humility are the very cream, the very essence of pride; the really humble person wishes to be, and not to appear so. Humility is timorous, and starts at her shadow; and so delicate that if she hears her name pronounced it endangers her existence."[14]

In contrast, he declared, pride is so pervasive that it "dies twenty minutes after death."[15] Even displeasure at our own behavior can be a matter of pride. "Fits of anger, vexation, and bitterness against ourselves tend to pride and they spring from no other source than self-love, which is disturbed and upset at seeing that it is imperfect."[16]

What are some of the forms our pride takes? Haughtiness over our knowledge or our intelligence (intellectual pride); over our gifts (physical beauty, athletic or vocational skills); over our accomplishments; even over our spiritual progress in devotion (spiritual pride). It also comes out in our driving aggressively, impatiently, or competitively. This is a most popular expression of pride (to which I have succumbed too often).

Of course, one needs to be humble enough to say, "I have a problem. I have thoughts or ideas that are sinful." If we can't say that, we can't benefit from a book on overcoming sinful thoughts.

## Examples of the Saints

The saints did more than talk about humility; they put it into practice and so became models for us to emulate. St. John Vianney

[14] Jean Pierre Camus, *The Spirit of St. Francis de Sales* (N.p.: Franklin Classics, 2018), 9.

[15] Attributed to Francis de Sales; source unknown.

[16] St. Francis de Sales, *Introduction to the Devout Life*, trans. John K. Ryan (New York: Image Books, 1986), 249.

showed his humility once when he received (by mistake) a petition circulated by his fellow priests accusing him of "sensationalism, ignorance, and [showy] poverty." He signed it and sent it on to the diocese. At one point he said, "I thought a time would come when people would run me out of Ars with sticks, when the bishop would suspend me, and I should end my days in prison. I see, however, that I am not worthy of such a grace."[17]

In 1841, he got a letter from a fellow priest who was more than twenty years younger (John Vianney was fifty-four at the time). It began, "Monsieur le Curé, when a man knows as little theology as you he ought never to enter a confessional." He went on to insult John in all sorts of ways. John wrote him back, saying,

> How many reasons I have to love you my dear and honored co-worker. You are the only person who really knows me. Since you are so good and charitable to take an interest in my poor soul, help me to obtain the grace I have asked for so long—that of being replaced in a position I am unworthy to fulfill because of my ignorance—so that I may be able to retire into some corner, there to weep over my poor life.... How much penance I must do, how many tears to shed!

When the priest received John's reply, he walked to Ars and "threw himself" at the saint's feet to ask forgiveness.[18]

Near the end of his life, St. John of the Cross developed an inflammation in his foot that caused him to have a fever. The

---

[17] Abbé Francis Trochu, *The Curé d'Ars* (Rockford, IL: TAN Books, 1977), 178, 174.

[18] Alfred Monnin, *The Curé of Ars*, trans. Bertram Wolferstam, SJ (Saint Louis: Herder, 1924), 206–207.

prior thought of sending him to the town of Baeza, where he could be treated by doctors and where he was highly thought of. But John asked to be sent to Úbeda, where he would not be treated with great respect. The prior at Úbeda was Francisco Crisóstomo, a harsh man who had no use for those considered to be holy. Furthermore, he had never forgiven John for having corrected him years earlier for long absences from the priory. So he gave John the most miserable room in the priory. And when John was kept by his illness from being able to get to the dining room one day, Crisóstomo demanded that John come to him, whereupon he humiliated him by publicly scolding him.

Crisóstomo complained that the special food prescribed for John by the doctors was eating into the priory's finances, even though most of the food was donated by the people in the town. He would go each day to John's room and scold the sick man for his defects. And he would mock John for having corrected him years before. The prior would not allow anyone to visit John without his permission, and his final insult was to take away the friar taking care of him. The young friars were so scandalized by this that one of them reported Crisóstomo's cruelty to the provincial. The provincial came and scolded Crisóstomo for his shameful behavior. He stayed a few days to make sure John got better treatment.

Meanwhile, the doctor who dressed John's wound became convinced that John was a saint and saved the bandages as relics. A sweet-smelling aroma emanating from the bandages confirmed the doctor's opinion.

John's health worsened, and it became clear that he was nearing death. When Crisóstomo came to see him, John humbly requested pardon of the prior for being a burden to him. The prior was filled with guilt and self-reproach and asked forgiveness for treating him badly. He muttered that the monastery didn't have much money. John answered, "Father, I have been treated far better than I deserve. But do not be distressed by the poverty of the house for if you have faith in the Lord it will soon be relieved." (And it was.) As he left John's room, the prior could not hold back his tears.

From that day, Crisóstomo was a changed man. He returned later and begged on his knees to have John's breviary when he died. John replied, "I have nothing that belongs to me that I can give Your Reverence; everything is yours for you are my superior."[19]

Shortly thereafter, John died. Hundreds upon hundreds attended his funeral. His relics were brought to various parts of Spain. Many miracles occurred for those who touched them.

## David

Have you ever wondered how King David became a key figure in the Old Testament? After all, he was an adulterer and a murderer. Yet he was told that his son would have a strong kingdom and his throne would last forever:

> Thus says the Lord of hosts.... When your days have been completed and you rest with your ancestors, I will raise up your offspring after you, sprung from your loins, and I will establish his kingdom. He it is who shall build a house for my name, and I will establish his royal throne forever. I will be a father to him, and he shall be a son to me....

---

[19] Gerald Brenan, *St. John of the Cross: His Life and Poetry* (London: Cambridge University Press, 1973), 78–80.

Your house and your kingdom are firm forever before me;
your throne shall be firmly established forever. (2 Sam.
7:12–14, 16, NABRE)

How did he qualify for that honor, in light of his sins? Because
of his *humility*. When the prophet Nathan accused David with
a blistering account of his sins, David replied, "I have sinned
against the Lord" (2 Sam. 12:13). Psalm 51 is said to be David's
humble prayer for mercy before God:

Have mercy on me, O God,
according to your steadfast love;
according to your abundant mercy
blot out my transgressions.
Wash me thoroughly from my iniquity,
and cleanse me from my sin.

For I know my transgressions,
and my sin is ever before me.
Against you, you alone, have I sinned,
and done what is evil in your sight,
so that you are justified in your sentence
and blameless when you pass judgment.
Indeed, I was born guilty,
a sinner when my mother conceived me.

You desire truth in the inward being;
therefore teach me wisdom in my secret
heart.
Purge me with hyssop, and I shall be clean;
wash me, and I shall be whiter than snow.
Let me hear joy and gladness;
let the bones that you have crushed rejoice.

# Overcoming Sinful Thoughts

Hide your face from my sins,
    and blot out all my iniquities.

Create in me a clean heart, O God,
    and put a new and right spirit within me.
Do not cast me away from your presence,
    and do not take your holy spirit from me.
Restore to me the joy of your salvation,
    and sustain in me a willing spirit.

Then I will teach transgressors your ways,
    and sinners will return to you.
Deliver me from bloodshed, O God,
    O God of my salvation,
    and my tongue will sing aloud of your
    deliverance.

O Lord, open my lips,
    and my mouth will declare your praise.
For you have no delight in sacrifice;
    if I were to give a burnt offering, you would not be
    pleased.
The sacrifice acceptable to God is a broken spirit;
    a broken and contrite heart, O God, you will not
    despise. (Ps. 51:1–17)

Humility personified. That great humility, even after his mortal sins, is what obtained for David the privilege of being the great-great- … great-grandfather of Jesus. Jesus was often called "Son of David," implying that He was the fulfillment of the promise to David: He was the Messiah. In fact, when the crowds called Him that in the temple area, the chief priests and the scribes were indignant, since they knew that the crowds were in effect calling Him the Messiah.

Our blessed Lord makes it clear in the Gospel of Luke that spiritual pride can bring down a person practicing religion, whereas humility can lift up a sinner:

> [Jesus] also told this parable to some who trusted in them-
> selves that they were righteous and despised others: "Two
> men went up into the temple to pray, one a Pharisee and
> the other a tax collector. The Pharisee, standing by him-
> self, prayed thus: 'God, I thank you that I am not like other
> men, extortioners, unjust, adulterers, or even like this tax
> collector. I fast twice a week; I give tithes of all that I get.'
> But the tax collector, standing far off, would not even lift
> up his eyes to heaven, but beat his breast, saying, 'God, be
> merciful to me, a sinner!' I tell you, this man went down to
> his house justified, rather than the other; for everyone who
> exalts himself will be humbled, but the one who humbles
> himself will be exalted." (Luke 18:10–14, RSV)

What an extraordinary message! The Pharisee fasted twice a week and gave 10 percent of his income to the poor or to the church. Tax collectors were known to extort more taxes than were due, keeping the extra for themselves. It was considered a scandal among the Jews for someone to marry into a family with a tax collector in it. Tax collectors were seen as the scum of the earth. Yet Jesus said the tax collector was, in a sense, better off than the Pharisee, who practiced his faith but fell into spiritual pride. The tax collector's humility was his saving grace.

I am sure this parable shook the people listening to Jesus. It should shake us as well. God wants no part in our pride, spiritual or otherwise. How vitally important it is to pray for and strive for the preeminent virtue of humility!

## Mary

There should be no doubt that the most humble of all the saints was Blessed Mary. St. Alphonsus Liguori wrote:

> "Humility," says St. Bernard, "is the foundation and guardian of virtues;" and with reason, for without it no other virtue can exist in a soul. Should she possess all virtues, all will depart when humility is gone. But, on the other hand, as St. Francis de Sales wrote to St. Jane Frances de Chantal, "God so loves humility, that whenever He sees it, He is immediately drawn there...." Mary, being the first and most perfect disciple of Jesus Christ in the practice of all virtues, was the first also in that of humility, and by it merited to be exalted above all creatures. It was revealed to St. Matilda that the first virtue in which the Blessed Mother particularly exercised herself, from her very childhood, was that of humility....
>
> St. Bernardine says, that "after the Son of God, no creature in the world was so exalted as Mary, because no creature in the world ever humbled itself so much as she did."[20]

Humility ranks with love as a virtue that Jesus invited us to imitate: "Learn from me, for I am gentle and humble in heart, and

[20] St. Alphonsus Liguori, *The Glories of Mary* (London: Burns and Oates, 1858).

you will find rest for your souls" (Matt. 11:29). Don't leave home without it!

## Prayer for Humility

A litany for humility is attributed to Cardinal Merry del Val, secretary of state for Pope St. Pius X. What follows is an adaptation of that prayer, shortened to encourage daily recitation:

> O Jesus! meek and humble of heart,
> make my heart like unto Thine.
>
> From the desire to be esteemed, *deliver me*.
> From the desire to be honored, *deliver me*.
> From the desire to be praised, *deliver me*.
>
> Teach me to accept humiliation,
> contempt, rebukes,
> being slandered, being ignored,
> being insulted, being wronged,
> and being belittled.
>
> Jesus, grant me the grace
> that others be admired more than I;
> that others be praised and I unnoticed;
> that others be preferred to me in everything;
> that others be holier than I,
> provided I become as holy as I should;
> that I might imitate the patience and obedience
> of Your mother, Mary. Amen.

2

# "I Need to Succeed at All Costs"

The story of ancient Israel is one of repeated cycles of success, taking God for granted, crashing down, and then reforming. We could begin with the Exodus of the Israelites from their slavery in Egypt around the twelfth century BC. God provided water, manna, and even quail for them in the desert. They still complained, so God punished them with serpents whose bites made them ill and killed some of them. After this, the Israelites repented of their complaining and lack of trust. They admitted their sin and asked Moses to pray that the Lord would get rid of the snakes. Of course, there remained the problem of those who were already sick. So the Lord had Moses mount a bronze snake on a pole. Whoever looked upon this serpent would be healed.[21] Success; turning from God; crashing down; and reform.

We should expect the same cycle in our own lives. We can hope to experience success, but life will not be all roses. God knows that failure can get our attention, spurring us to reform.

---

[21] The serpent was a symbol of Jesus, lifted on the Cross, appearing venomous but bringing healing to those who looked upon Him with faith. (It would also become the symbol for the medical profession.)

## Israel's Travails

The history of Israel's successes and failures continues. David became king of Israel after many military successes. He decided to take a census of his troops even though he was warned by Joab that God was against this. The Lord gave him a choice of three calamities as a punishment. David chose a plague, which caused the death of seventy thousand men. He humbled himself before God and was forgiven.

Some time later, while his soldiers were off fighting battles for Israel, he committed adultery with Bathsheba and then had her husband murdered. He received his punishment, repented, and then flourished again.

Then Solomon succeeded David and had a peaceful and thriving kingdom. However, despite the warnings in Deuteronomy—the king "must not acquire many wives for himself, or else his heart will turn away; also silver and gold he must not acquire in great quantity for himself" (Deut. 17:17)—he did both of these things. 1 Kings 11 spells out what else he did against the will of God. He married many foreign women even though the Lord had told the Israelites not to do so "for they will surely incline your heart to follow their gods." He had seven hundred wives and three hundred concubines! They led him to worship foreign gods. "His heart was not true to the Lord his God, as was the heart of his father David" (1 Kings 11:2, 4).

For all this evil, the Lord told Solomon, "Since this has been your mind and you have not kept my covenant and my statutes that I have commanded you, I will surely tear the kingdom from you and give it to your servant. Yet for the sake of your father David I will not do it in your lifetime; I will tear it out of the hand of your son" (1 Kings 11:11–12).

Uzziah came to power in Judah, by then split from Israel, in about 791 BC. He won wars against other countries, brought prosperity to his nation, and rebuilt the walls of Jerusalem. He built up a large army and expanded Judah to the west. He directed water conservation to make desert areas usable again. His success was attributed to his fidelity to the Lord God.

Alas, he became proud because of his great prosperity. He violated Temple rules and tried to burn incense in the Temple, something reserved for the priests alone. When the priests tried to get him to leave, he became livid, at which point he was afflicted with leprosy. That ended his reign (2 Chron. 26:16–21). Success had led to failure, as it so often does.

### Secular Dangers

This pattern is not restricted to salvation history. There are pitfalls for our successes in the secular world as well. When we achieve success, we tend to believe all the adulation we begin to receive. We fall into pride, the worst of the seven deadly sins. Then we tend to dismiss those who challenge us. We may try to surround ourselves with yes-men, those who go along with us at every turn. Then we become isolated from potentially helpful critics. We fall into narcissism, where we are the measure of everything. What follows is often failure.[22]

We can thus see how this sinful thought is linked to the thought of the previous chapter: pride. Although it is not wrong to acknowledge that we did something well, it is wrong to take all the credit. We need not deny our successes, but we

---

[22] Vince Miller, "The 5 Hidden Dangers of Success," Resolute, July 10, 2018, https://beresolute.org/the-5-hidden-dangers-of-success/.

should acknowledge God's guidance, and the aid we received from those who made our successes possible. A person might answer, "Look, I worked very hard on this. I used my experience, my creativity, and my cleverness and got it done. Why should I give God credit?" Well, where did you get the health and strength to work hard? To gain experience? Where did you learn to be creative? Was it by accident, or did you have some guidance? Did you learn to be clever by reading something, or did you learn from another clever person? Did you find that article by accident or meet that person by accident, or were you led to them?

The story is told of a farmer who asked his pastor to come and bless his farm. He had bought it several years before and had worked very hard to fix up his farmhouse and plant crops. As he showed him around, the pastor commented on the farmer's accomplishments. "You and God have done a great job on renovating this house"; "You and God have done wonderful work on this corn field. That's the tallest corn I have ever seen"; "You and God have produced an abundance of blueberries here."

Finally, the farmer blurted out, "Pastor, you should have seen this place when God had it all to himself!" The point is, the farmer deserved some credit but the pastor was right: he didn't deserve *all* the credit.

Pastor Jim Wiegand wrote, "The fastest way to see God's blessings leave what I'm doing is to take credit for what He's doing. A blessed AND humble leader is one of the greatest balancing acts in the world."[23]

[23] Quoted in John Opalewski, "3 Hidden Dangers of Success" Converge Coaching, September 8, 2017, https://convergecoach. com/3-hidden-dangers-of-success/.

T. J. Tison, a blogger at *Working Women of Faith*, tells of her interview with a businessman:

> I recently sat down with a seasoned believer who owns an incredibly successful business. I asked him what three things he learned through being a life-long business owner. Being on the other side of his life's work he had a clarity of vision that we don't often have in the middle of our careers. He is a strong believer and a wise man, and here is his first thing:
>
> "I didn't always give God the credit."
>
> He tended to think that it was his hard work and efforts that brought him success and didn't look at God as the answer. But now, looking back over his life, he can see God's influence on his business. He can trace back through the years God's direction, path to success, protection from harm and errors, and how it was God that did all of the work that brought him success.[24]

We read in Sacred Scripture, "Not to us, O LORD, not to us, but to your name give glory, for the sake of your steadfast love and your faithfulness" (Ps. 115:1). St. Paul writes, "What have you that you did not receive? If then you received it, why do you boast as if it were not a gift?" (1 Cor. 4:7). And elsewhere he says, "Not that we are competent of ourselves to claim anything as coming from us; our competence is from God" (2 Cor. 3:5). That should be our motto as we pursue success in the world or in our church: our competence is from God.

---

[24] T. J. Tison, "Giving God the Credit," *Working Women of Faith* (blog), https://workingwomenoffaith.com/giving-god-the-credit/.

## Success Attachment

Perhaps the greatest danger in success is becoming attached to it. We feel that we must hang on to our success in order to be happy. In fact, we Christians should know that to be happy we need God and whatever He gives us for the moment.

When we become attached to our success, we might be tempted to pay for continued success—and pay too much. We might pursue immoral means to keep it.

One saint comes to mind. When Margaret of Cortona was young, she was extremely beautiful and quite spirited. Unfortunately, her father spoiled her on the one hand and had a violent temper on the other. As a result, she sought love outside her home. Because she was so attractive, the boys in her town could not get enough of her. Alas, she loved the attention and was willing to pay for it by giving in to their immoral desires. By age seventeen, her unchaste activity was known by all in the town. Beautiful women without loving fathers, beware.

Happily, Margaret had a huge conversion and lived so devoutly from age twenty-seven until her death that she became a saint.

The obsession with worldly success penetrated deeply into the sports world in the late 1960s. Al Oerter, discus champion at four straight Olympics ending in 1968, claimed that the Olympics turned "chemical" at the end of his career. Parents would approach him and ask what sort of steroids or human growth hormone they should put their child on to improve their performances. Success at all costs.

In 1968, the International Olympic Committee established drug testing for the first time. Only one athlete was disqualified. In 1972, seven were disqualified. Four years later, eleven were disqualified. The use of drugs spread to horse racing, baseball, cycling, hockey, and football in the years that followed.

A 2007 study of fifty-two German athletes given anabolic steroids in the 1970s and 1980s without their knowledge showed some gruesome results. A quarter of them had cancer; one-third had considered suicide; miscarriage or stillbirth in the women was thirty-two times higher than average. Of sixty-nine children of these athletes who survived, seven had physical deformities and four were mentally challenged.[25]

These statistics show the natural results of pursuing success at all costs. The spiritual damage is even greater. How important it is for Christians—and everyone else—to be aware of the dangers of "success attachment." This can afflict us even in our religious and evangelization successes. The most important thing in life is not success but being faithful to the Lord, and of course, giving Him credit for empowering us to be successful. But God is not nearly so concerned with our success—even in our prayer life—as with our effort, made in and for Him. According to the well-known phrase of St. Teresa of Calcutta, our primary goal is "faithfulness, not success."

## Success for My Team!

A corollary to the "success at all costs" mentality is sports attachment. Some years back, I attended a priest retreat given by Fr. Angelus Shaughnessy, OFM Cap., during which he mentioned that he had been a great fan of the Pittsburgh Steelers. He had to

---

[25] "History of Performance Enhancing Drugs in Sports," Britannica ProCon, April 16, 2020, https://sportsanddrugs.procon.org/view. timeline.php?timelineID=000017.

watch every game and would stay up late to watch if they played late. He said that he realized that this was an attachment,[26] a detriment to his spiritual life, so he decided to stop watching the Steelers entirely.

There are some—mostly men—who feel they *need* to watch their sports team no matter what. If there is a wedding, a family reunion, or a fiftieth wedding anniversary, they must skip at least part of those events to watch their favorite team's game. Some want to watch *every* (mostly football) game on TV. That is attachment, bordering on addiction.

Now, one might ask why it is good to watch sports at all. There are two reasons. First, it is entertaining, a kind of recreation. It is healthy to get our minds off our work and other obligations and do something enjoyable. Second, by following our local team and talking sports with our friends and acquaintances, we build a little solidarity. It has the effect of drawing the community together and forming friendships. Friendship is important for our well-being. St. Thomas Aquinas wrote, "There is nothing on this earth more to be prized than true friendship."[27]

Watching sports is like pursuing any form of entertainment. If we are desperate to have it and feel we cannot live without it, that is disordered. Every worldly attachment draws us away from our best attachment, God. Granted, sports attachment is less harmful than substance addiction, but it can still be an obstacle to the spiritual life.[28]

---

[26] An attachment is something or someone you feel you must have to be happy.

[27] *De Regno* (*On Kingship, to the King of Cyprus*), bk. 1, chap. 11, no. 77.

[28] St. John of the Cross wrote, "Hence, we call this nakedness [this mortification of appetites] a night for the soul, for we are

Something similar may be said about playing sports. To admit being a tennis nut or a golf nut is to admit excess. It's fine to play tennis or golf two or three times a week as long as these things don't cut into our family or work obligations. In fact, doing so can be beneficial to mental and physical health.

One way to be truly detached from sports, and save some souls as well, is to have a day (especially Friday) when you don't follow sports at all. You don't watch; you don't listen; you don't check the scores from the night before. You celebrate a sports blackout. For me, that is harder than fasting from food, which I do as well on Fridays.

So, enjoy sports, but don't let them — or any other entertainment — dominate your life.

---

not discussing the mere lack of things; this lack will not divest the soul if it craves for all these objects. We are dealing with the [emptying] of the soul's appetites and gratifications. This is what leaves it free and empty of all things, even though it possesses them. Since the things of the world cannot enter the soul, they are not in themselves an encumbrance or harm to it; rather, it is the will and appetite dwelling within that causes the damage when set on these things." *Ascent of Mount Carmel*, bk. 1, chap. 3.

3

# "I Deserve Everything I Have"

Some years ago, Fr. William Byron, former president of Catholic University, gave a talk in which he stated that the sense of entitlement is the dominant trait among students today. He said:

> Once we put ourselves in the thanks-saying, thank-giving, thanks-doing mood, as we are right now, it is a good idea to pay attention to a rising sense of entitlement in America, especially among the young. And I would suggest to you today that ingratitude is the infrastructure of entitlement.
>
> Think about that—ingratitude is the infrastructure of entitlement, and entitlement is our cultural condition of thinking we deserve everything we have. Entitlement prompts us to make demands, not to give thanks.[29]

Ingratitude is a trait detrimental to human fulfillment. In her 2015 article "So THIS Is Why Gratitude Makes Us Happier," author Kaia Roman wrote how becoming grateful helped her get out of her depression:

[29] William J. Byron, SJ, "Much Obliged—Gratitude without Entitlement" (keynote address, alumni/father-son Communion breakfast, St. Joseph's Preparatory School, Philadelphia, February 24, 2013), http://amdg44.blogspot.com/.

After sinking into depression last year, I was so desperate to free myself that I tried anything and everything I could. I'd heard that frequent gratitude can increase happiness, but I didn't really know why — other than the obvious: If you focus on what you are grateful for, you'll likely realize that your troubles aren't as bad as they seem.

But that was good enough for me, so I grabbed onto gratitude like a life raft, and it pulled me out of one of the lowest times in my life.... Having a regular gratitude practice was and continues to be a key component of my "joy plan."

Roman did some research and found that the brain sees gratitude as optimism, which calms the amygdala, the segment of the brain that signals stress. It also reduces the stress hormone cortisol, releases pleasure-inducing neurotransmitters, and stimulates the parasympathetic nervous system, producing a calming effect.

Roman recommends starting a gratitude notebook and scheduling time each morning to write in it. If the notebook would be too much, she recommends just thinking of some things each day for which you are grateful. She also suggests telling others how grateful you are for them. It will help them feel good and will have a good effect on *you* as well.

Studies have shown that Roman's success in ending depression through gratitude was not unique. As gratitude increases in a person, depression decreases. Clinical psychologist Philip Watkins at Eastern Washington University discovered that those who were clinically depressed manifested almost 50 percent less gratitude than controls who were not depressed.[30]

[30] Ocean Robbins, "The Neuroscience of Why Gratitude Makes Us Healthier," Daily Good, October 30, 2013, http://www.

Other university studies confirm the positive effects of gratitude. In one study, researchers formed three groups randomly,
giving each a task. One group was to record five things they were
grateful for in the preceding week. The second was to write down
five negative things they experienced in the previous week, and
the third was to write about anything that they had dealt with
in the previous week, good or bad. After ten weeks, the gratitude
group reported being 25 percent happier than the negative group.
Their health condition was better, and they spent 1.5 hours more
in exercising per week.

Another study had people write *daily* about things they were
grateful for. The benefits were even greater than for those who
reported their blessing weekly. In addition, the gratitude group
offered more emotional support for those in need.

A third study focused on adults who had neuromuscular dis-
orders (NMDs). The gratitude writers were able to sleep longer
hours and awakened more refreshed. They were better satisfied
with their lives, more optimistic, and felt closer to others than
the control group that did not write.

The improvements observed in these studies were not felt
only by the participants; others also noticed their improvement.
Researchers discovered that "spouses of the participants in the
gratitude (group) reported that the participants appeared to have
higher subjective well-being than did the spouses of the participants in the control (group)."

John Gottman, marriage researcher at the University of
Washington, wrote that, to ensure a healthy marriage, couples

dailygood.org/story/578/the-neuroscience-of-why-gratitude-
makes-us-healthier/. All of the following quotations and studies
cited in this section are taken from this article.

must have five positive interactions for every negative. Negative interactions would include hot arguments, criticism, rolling of the eyes, complaints, or put-downs. Positives would include praise, hugs, thank-yous, warm smiles, and sharing laughter. A thank-you, as we have seen, is a blessing for both the thanker and the "thankee."

## Thanksgiving in Scripture

Giving thanks is big in Sacred Scripture. For example, Paul tells us, "Give thanks in all circumstances; for this is the will of God in Christ Jesus for you" (1 Thess. 5:18). Psalm 136 begins with these verses:

> O give thanks to the LORD, for he is good,
>   for his steadfast love endures forever.
> O give thanks to the God of gods,
>   for his steadfast love endures forever.
> O give thanks to the LORD of lords,
>   for his steadfast love endures forever.

So we have three thank-yous (three such positives represent a superlative in biblical language) for the enduring love of God (*hesed* in Hebrew). This is followed by twenty-two verses of why we are giving thanks — what God has done for His people — and then another "Give thanks" to God for His love.

The angel Raphael said to Tobiah and Tobit, "Bless God and give him thanks before all the living for the good things he has done for you, by blessing and extolling his name in song. Proclaim before all with due honor the deeds of God, and do not be slack in thanking him" (Tobit 12:6, NABRE). Words such as *thanks* and *thanksgiving* appear about 260 times in Sacred Scripture.

And the word *Eucharist* means "thanksgiving." In America, the fourth Thursday of November is set aside as a day to give thanks. Christians (and Americans) are a thankful people.

I asked a person once to thank God for three or four things each day. She asked, "What should I thank Him for?" I answered, "How about for living in America rather than in the Middle East; or for having a roof over your head, food to eat, a vehicle to drive, friends, good relatives, air to breathe ..."

St. Thérèse of Lisieux told her sister Céline, "Gratitude is the thing that brings us the most grace.... I am content with whatever God gives me, and I show Him this in a thousand little ways."[31] When Céline entered the Carmelites, she asked Thérèse to write a poem indicating all she had sacrificed for God by entering the convent. Thérèse wrote her a poem, but in it, she thanked Jesus for what He had given her.

When I entered the seminary, I figured I was giving up a lot to serve the Lord as a priest. After some years as a priest, I realize that the priesthood was God's superabundant gift *to me*.

Let us give thanks to the Lord for He is good; His mercy endures forever.

## Prayer of Thanksgiving

Heavenly Father,
Thank You for my very existence
which You gave me out of the abundance of Your love
and which You sustain at every moment.

---

[31] Quoted in Christopher O'Mahony, *St. Thérèse of Lisieux: Testimonies from the Process of Beatification* (Ann Arbor: University of Michigan, 1975), 138.

# Overcoming Sinful Thoughts

Thank You for my health,
which I so often take for granted,
for my family, which I also take for granted.

Thank You for my intellect,
by which You enable me to think,
and for my will, by which You enable me to love.

Thank You for my body,
and the food and drink by which You sustain it,
and the shelter by which You protect it.

Thank You for my soul,
and the grace of Your Holy Spirit
by which You nourish it.

My every talent comes from You,
my every possession,
my every moment,
for which I will be eternally grateful.

Thank You for Blessed Mary,
who intercedes for me before You.
And thank You most of all for Jesus,
who has given us new life, new hope, new love
by His death and Resurrection,
and for the Church, which brings Him to us each day.
What an awesome, generous, loving God You are!

You ask me to worship You at least weekly
and to pray to You without ceasing.
It is my privilege and my joy to do so
in thanksgiving for all You have given me. Amen.

4

# "God Doesn't Hear My Prayers;
# Why Bother?"

"I have prayed about this for so long. God doesn't hear me. Or at least He doesn't listen!" If you say this, you are not alone. The psalmist had the same problem.

> Why, O Lord, do you stand far off?
> Why do you hide yourself in times of trouble? (Ps. 10:1)

So how can we get God to answer our prayers? Jesus said:

> Abide in me as I abide in you. Just as the branch cannot bear fruit by itself unless it abides in the vine, neither can you unless you abide in me. I am the vine, you are the branches. Those who abide in me and I in them bear much fruit, because apart from me you can do nothing.... If you abide in me, and my words abide in you, ask for whatever you wish, and it will be done for you. My Father is glorified by this, that you bear much fruit and become my disciples. (John 15:4–5, 7–8)

If we think about it, we should realize that abiding in Jesus and having His words abide in us is a tall order. To abide in Jesus means to live in the state of grace—and more: it means, in a sense, to live and breathe Jesus Christ, to make Him the measure of everything we think and do.

Although it is true that God sometimes answers the prayers of sinners to turn them back from their sinful ways, He is far more likely to answer the prayers of someone who loves Him a great deal. "We know that all things work together for good for those who love God" (Rom. 8:28). And, "See, the Lord's hand is not too short to save, nor his ear too dull to hear. Rather, your iniquities have been barriers between you and your God, and your sins have hidden his face from you so that he does not hear" (Isa. 59:1–2).

So what does this mean for your prayer life? It means asking for intimacy with God above all and asking everything according to God's will. "If we ask anything according to his will, he hears us" (1 John 5:14). Is it okay to ask for the healing of a loved one? Yes, but always add, "Thy will be done" and trust that God always wills what is good. Remember the prayer of Jesus in the Garden of Gethsemane: "Father, if you are willing, remove this cup from me; yet, not my will but yours be done" (Luke 22:42). That is the classic way to pray for relief from trials. Ask for what you want, but affirm that you want God's will to be done.

We are warned in James about praying for the wrong things: "You ask and do not receive, because you ask wrongly, in order to spend what you get on your pleasures" (James 4:3). The disciples were deterred from their desire to take revenge on the Samaritans who refused to welcome them: " 'Lord, do you want us to command fire to come down from heaven and consume them?' But he turned and rebuked them" (Luke 9:54–55).

St. Monica prayed for her cohabiting son, Augustine, for seventeen years. Early on, she went to her bishop and asked in tears why her son had not reformed. He replied, "It is not possible that the son of so many tears should perish. Your son will be saved." Augustine did convert to Christianity and became a priest, then a bishop, and ultimately a saint. He is the most quoted saint in the history of the Catholic Church.

I had a parishioner who prayed for the conversion of her father for twenty-five years. He converted on his deathbed.

Some people who pray expect God to answer every prayer with a yes. If they don't get a positive answer, they stop praying or going to church. You can't manipulate God. He won't say yes to every prayer. Sometimes he says no, but every answer He gives is for our good.

## The Prayer of Children

If you want to get God's attention, get your young children to pray. Years ago, a young teaching sister told me of her first graders' prayer experience. They needed a rug for activities for which they had to sit on the floor, so she got them all to pray for the rug. Within a few days, some workmen, who knew nothing of their prayers, walked in with a rug and said, "We are getting rid of this. Can you use it somewhere?" The children were delighted to see their prayer answered so quickly. It was a boost to their faith.

Sister decided to keep the magic going. Johnny's father had been out of work for a couple of months, so the whole class prayed for him to get a job. In less than a week, he had a job.

When I had my knee replaced, I asked the first and second graders in our parish school to pray that I would be able to play tennis again by May. I promised to buy pizza for both classes if I were able to play. It looked as if it would not happen, but an old partner called me the last week in May, and we played a couple of days later. The children got the pizza. I won the tennis match. (Full disclosure: my opponent was also recovering from an injury.)

Our parish's world-class youth minister asked me one day if I was praying for her. I said, "Yes, every day." She asked, "Are you praying that I find a good husband?"

"No," I responded.

"Why not?" she asked earnestly.

"Because if you get married, you will start having children and we will lose the best youth minister we ever had," I answered whimsically.

"Father, you've gotta pray for me!"

"Okay, okay, I will," I conceded reluctantly.

Some months later, she left our parish to take a job at another parish. On her final day, I handed out thirty prayer cards to the youth-group members with a prayer to St. Anthony to find her a worthy Catholic husband. One of the adult leaders showed her the card, and she came over and asked me, "Father, what have you done? This is so embarrassing!"

I responded, "If it works it will be okay, no?" She admitted, "I guess it would be."

It worked. A month later, she met a good Catholic man, a daily communicant. A year and a half later, they got married. At the end of the nuptial Mass, I told the story and proclaimed, "Nice job, St. Anthony!"

My former roommate married a young woman who was one of twelve children. Talking to them at their wedding, I discovered that just about all of the siblings prayed the Rosary and attended Mass daily. I asked one of them how he would explain that. He responded, "When we were kids, we would all pray for a special intention and the answer was usually yes. So we learned the power of prayer."

If you want a good answer to prayer, get your kids to pray.

## Prayer of a Single Christian

I have been working with young adults for many years, and it has become clear that it is common for Catholics of that age to stress out over what their vocation is. "I am getting older. Will I ever be married?" So I wrote them a prayer to say:

> Lord, I think perhaps You want me to marry, but I'm not sure. I know it's better to be single and wish you were married than to be married and wish you were single, but I'd really like to be married. However, if that's not what You want, Lord, then I'll go with that all the way, because I trust You. And I believe that my vocation today is to be single, and that this is not some accident of the laws of probability but the thing You want for me today, my true calling for now, something You planned for me for all eternity. One thing is certain: my vocation is to love You and be with You and to find happiness in You above all, now and in the future; and You alone can make me happy. So, I am going to use my time to draw close to You, even if that limits my possibility of marrying, because marriage without You, Lord, would be tragic. May I never settle for anyone but one who will help me live in You.

One anxious single Catholic wrote to tell me, "If I pray that prayer, I will never be married." My response: "But you will be holy ... and happy." Being holy and happy makes one far more marriageable. Being willing to give up our most precious desire for God is a sign of true holiness. It is the sacrifice of Abraham.

Speaking of holiness, that is a wonderful precondition for receiving a positive answer to our prayers. Think of the saints who were able to work so many miracles for those who came to them for healing. St. Bernard of Clairvaux performed countless miracles, including fifteen in one day; St. John Vianney saw many healings in those who prayed, at his suggestion, to his favorite saint, St. Philomena; St. John Bosco performed so many miracles that Pius XI declared, "In the life of John Bosco the supernatural and the miraculous became ordinary."[32]

Some Christian writers urge us to confess our sins to get a better hearing for our prayers. Catholics have a wonderful sacrament available in which we receive confirmation of God's merciful forgiveness. The closer we are to God, the more likely our prayers will be answered—and the more in tune with God's will our prayers will be.

## Choose Your Intentions Well

Not every prayer intention is likely to receive a positive answer. In college, I met a wonderful young woman and started to pray that we would end up together. Then I realized I needed to give God some more room in this endeavor, so I changed my intention and prayed that it would work out for us but that if it was not God's will, He would make it clear. It wasn't His will. And He made it clear. It was painful but, in retrospect, good.

[32] Quoted in "St. John Bosco," EWTN, https://www.ewtn.com/catholicism/saints/john-bosco-631.

When I turned thirty-one, I said to myself, "Self, you are not getting any younger. You had better crank up the prayer for your vocation"—which I was certain was marriage. So I began to say two or three Rosaries a day, and after a few months, I began to attend daily Mass. By this time, it occurred to me that I should just ask God to show me my vocation and not pray to meet Miss Right. I was thirty-three when I got my answer. To my utter surprise, it became clear that my vocation was to the priesthood!

When this conviction entered my mind with some force, I asked, "Lord, are You sure? I've been looking for a wife." He was sure. The idea stayed with me, and from the time I said yes (at age thirty-four; I was ordained five years later) I have been happy—*very* happy.

There is a wonderful poem, allegedly written by an unknown Confederate soldier, about how God gives us something much better than what we pray for:

> I asked for strength that I might achieve;
> I was made weak that I might learn humbly to obey.
> I asked for health that I might do greater things;
> I was given infirmity that I might do better things.
> I asked for riches that I might be happy;
> I was given poverty that I might be wise.
> I asked for power that I might have the praise of men;
> I was given weakness that I might feel the need of God.
> I asked for all things that I might enjoy life;
> I was given life that I might enjoy all things.
> I got nothing that I had asked for,
> but everything that I had hoped for.
> Almost despite myself my unspoken prayers were
>     answered;
> I am, among all men, most richly blessed.

## Favorite Saint

Everyone should have a favorite saint whom they can call on for special needs. I pray to St. Anthony, not only to find things (and he is amazing at that) but for everything, including to remember things, to make my phone work, and for good weather.

Once I was playing tennis and the sky turned dark and the wind increased. I suggested to my partner, who is not Catholic, "Let's pray to St. Anthony that it doesn't rain till after we finish." "Good idea," he responded. It was about 2:00 when we made that prayer, and we were scheduled to play until 2:30. We finished playing at 2:30 exactly, and it started raining at 2:32. Nice going, St. Anthony!

St. Anthony seems to answer my prayers to him (or, to be precise, for his intercession) about 80 percent of the time. If you can get that percentage of positive responses by praying to a saint, you should count yourself blessed, and you should stay with that saint.[33]

## Prayer Motives

Many of us learned as children the four motives for prayer, summarized in the acronym, ACTS: adoration, contrition, thanksgiving, and supplication (or petition). All four of these are found in the classic prayers of the Church, the psalms.

### Adoration (Praise) Examples[34]

I will bless the LORD at all times;
  his praise shall continually be in my mouth....

---

[33] One person told me she was disappointed with God because He didn't answer her prayer. No loving father will answer every request. We cannot *control* God.

[34] See also Psalms 8; 100; 111; 145:21; 146, and 150, among others.

O magnify the LORD with me,
   and let us exalt his name together. (Ps. 34:1, 3)

Extol the LORD our God;
   worship at his footstool.
   Holy is he! (Ps. 99:5)

I will extol you, my God and King,
   and bless your name forever and ever.
Every day I will bless you,
   and praise your name forever and ever.
Great is the LORD, and greatly to be praised;
   his greatness is unsearchable. (Ps. 145:1–3)

### *Thanksgiving Examples*[35]

We will give thanks to your name forever. (Ps. 44:8)

O give thanks to the LORD, for he is good;
   for his steadfast love endures forever. (Ps. 106:1)

I give thanks to you, O LORD my God, with my
   whole heart,
   and I will glorify your name forever. (Ps. 86:12)

### *Contrition Examples*[36]

I confess my iniquity;
   I am sorry for my sin.
Those who are my foes without cause are mighty,
   and many are those who hate me wrongfully. (Ps.
38:18–19)

---

[35] See also Psalms 107:8, 9; 95:1–2; 100:4; and 118:19, among others.
[36] See also Psalms 6, 32, 102, 130, and 143.

Have mercy on me, O God,
  according to your steadfast love;
according to your abundant mercy
  blot out my transgressions.
Wash me thoroughly from my iniquity,
  and cleanse me from my sin. (Ps. 51:1–2)

*Supplication Examples*[37]

Incline Your ear, O Lord, and answer me;
For I am poor and needy.
Preserve my life, for I am devoted to you;
You are my God; be gracious to me, O Lord,
For to you do I cry all day long. (Ps. 86:1–3)

Hear my prayer, O Lord;
  give ear to my supplications in your faithfulness;
  answer me in your righteousness....
For the enemy has pursued me,
  crushing my life to the ground,
  making me sit in darkness like those long dead.
  (Ps. 143:1, 3)

The Our Father contains three of the four prayer motives: "hallowed be Thy name" (may your name be held holy — adoration); "Thy will be done ... give us this day our daily bread" (supplication); "forgive us our sins" (contrition); and "lead us not into temptation but deliver us from evil" (supplication).

The only thing missing in the Our Father is thanksgiving. But our greatest prayer, which is so much more than a prayer, is

---

[37] See also Psalms 4, 10, 13, 17, 22, 43, and 70, among others.

the Mass, and that is "super-thanksgiving." The word *Eucharist means* "thanksgiving."

## Divine Mercy Devotions

There are some very special prayers received by St. Maria Faustina in connection with the Divine Mercy devotion. She describes Jesus' instructions regarding one such prayer: "Call upon my mercy on behalf of sinners; I desire their salvation. When you say this prayer, with a contrite heart and with faith on behalf of some sinner, I will give him the grace of conversion. This is the prayer: O blood and water which gushed forth from the heart of Jesus as a fount of mercy for us, I trust in you."[38]

What an amazing promise! Notice, Jesus didn't say the person would be converted, but that the person would be given the *grace of conversion.* The person must embrace the grace and respond to it according to human freedom, but the Lord will make it easy. (The Marians—the congregation that promotes the Divine Mercy devotion—now recommend that this prayer be said three times before the Divine Mercy Chaplet.)

Regarding the chaplet, the Lord said, "Even if there were a sinner most hardened, if he were to recite this chaplet only once, he would receive grace from My infinite mercy." He added, "At the hour of their death, I defend as my own glory every soul that will say this chaplet; or when others say it for a dying person, the pardon is the same."[39]

There is another extraordinary promise related to the Divine Mercy devotion: the "prayer" of venerating the image of Divine

[38] *Diary,* nos. 186–187.
[39] *Diary,* nos. 687, 811.

Mercy. Our Blessed Lord said, "I promise that the soul that will venerate this image will not perish. I promise victory over [its] enemies already here on earth, especially at the hour of death. I myself will defend it as my own glory."[40]

Some time ago, I received a phone call from a friend in Seattle. He asked me to visit his mother-in-law in the hospital in Washington, DC. He told me, "I have no idea if she will welcome you or throw you out, but it would be great for her to have you visit her."

So I went. "Michelle" looked to be about eighty-five years old, and she had terminal cancer. She was really quite friendly, and we had a good conversation. When she said, "I am ready to go," I figured that would be a good time to work on her salvation.

I had brought with me a holy card with the Divine Mercy image on the front and the promise quoted above on the back. I encouraged Michelle to venerate it, and she seemed agreeable to doing so. I also gave her a leaflet on how to say the Divine Mercy Chaplet and asked her to say it once. She didn't say no. My request to her was based on the words of our Lord mentioned above regarding "a sinner most hardened."

Upon returning home, I e-mailed my friend to tell him about the visit. In his reply, he admitted that he was not sure that she had even been baptized. Then he wrote her saying that the only important thing in this life is to be saved, and that God is always ready to forgive all our sins if we only ask for His mercy.

I had planned to go back to see her in a week or two, but before I had a chance to do so, I received a call from my friend saying that she had been moved to another hospital's ICU because

---

[40] *Diary*, nos. 47–48.

her condition had worsened. I asked if any of her relatives were there with her so I could contact them. He said that her grand-daughter was there and gave me her cell phone number.

I asked the granddaughter to find out if Michelle had ever been baptized. She replied that she wasn't sure, perhaps not. I encouraged her to ask her grandmother if she wanted to be baptized. When Michelle said yes, I sent her granddaughter instructions on how to baptize her. It wasn't necessary. The hospital chaplain was on the ball and baptized her that same day. Michelle's daughter told me she had been urging Michelle to get baptized for decades, but she would never agree.

The next day I was able to get to the hospital to give Michelle First Holy Communion (after some catechizing) and Anointing of the Sick. She seemed most happy to receive these. I asked her if she had been venerating the holy card I gave her, and she smiled and said, "Oh yes." Meanwhile, her son-in-law had been saying a novena to Our Lady of Mount Carmel for her.

Just three or four weeks later, she died. It was a happy death. It seems that our Lord kept His promise. It seems likely that the fact that she had continued venerating the image was an important factor in her conversion. Were someone to kiss it once and throw it in the trash, this might not bring about the desired results. Also, the fact that she was over eighty and had terminal cancer no doubt expedited her conversion. There was little time for the Lord to fulfill His promise. If we were to give this holy card to someone much younger, it might take years, even decades, before that person would embrace the Faith.

In fact, I gave the same card to a middle-aged woman after the funeral of her father. "Linda" was Catholic but was not practicing the Faith. I asked her to venerate the card each day, and she said she would. When I saw her stepmother at Mass, I asked if Linda was still kissing the image, and she said she was. "But I can't get her to come to Mass," she added.

I responded, "Don't worry about that. God will work on her. He has plenty of time — she's only in her fifties. Just keep praying." Linda seems to be an example of one who will take some time to come around. Now I share this image and the message accompanying it with as many people as possible, including those who might share this with loved ones who are far from the Faith but have an affection for Jesus.

∞

We began by asking why God does not answer our prayers. It seems that our investigation has brought us to the point where, if we align ourselves to God's loving will, He *will* answer our prayers. This is because God is bound by His own goodness to give us what is best for us. So, as we reflect on prayer, we should come to pray less about receiving from God what *we* want and more about receiving from Him what *He* wants for us. Sure, we should still pray for what we want, but in the end, the best prayer is "Thy will be done."

## Best Prayers

Because they seek to align our will with God's, the following are some prayers that have a good chance of receiving a positive response. With all of these prayers, we should also spend time listening to God, by meditating on his Word, Jesus, to increase our hope for a good answer. If you want someone to answer your requests, you would do well to spend some quality and quantity time with him, and not just say hi or ask him for things from time to time.

*Lord, help me to know Your will and to carry it out.*
> Teach me to do your will,
>> for you are my God.
> Let your good spirit lead me
>> on a level path. (Ps. 143:10)

*Lord, enable me to be a witness of Your glory.*
> O give thanks to the Lord, call on his name,
>> make known his deeds among the peoples.
> Sing to him, sing praises to him,
>> tell of all his wonderful works. (1 Chron. 16:8–9)

*Lord, inspire me to forgive — and to love — my enemies.*
> If it is possible, so far as it depends on you, live peaceably with all. Beloved, never avenge yourselves, but leave room for the wrath of God; for it is written, "Vengeance is mine, I will repay, says the Lord." No, "if your enemies are hungry, feed them; if they are thirsty, give them something to drink." ... Do not be overcome by evil, but overcome evil with good. (Rom. 12:18–21)

*Lord, forgive me for my sins.*
> My little children, I am writing these things to you so that you may not sin. But if anyone does sin, we have an advocate with the Father, Jesus Christ the righteous. (1 John 2:1)

> In him we have redemption through his blood, the forgiveness of our trespasses, according to the riches of his grace. (Eph. 1:7)

# Overcoming Sinful Thoughts

*Lord help me to correct my brother diplomatically.*
Mortal, I have made you a sentinel for the house of Israel; whenever you hear a word from my mouth, you shall give them warning from me. If I say to the wicked, "You shall surely die," and you give them no warning, or speak to warn the wicked from their wicked way, in order to save their life, those wicked persons shall die for their iniquity; but their blood I will require at your hand. But if you warn the wicked, and they do not turn from their wickedness, or from their wicked way, they shall die for their iniquity; but you will have saved your life. (Ezek. 3:17–19)

*Lord, fill me with Your Holy Spirit.*
If you then, who are evil, know how to give good gifts to your children, how much more will the heavenly Father give the Holy Spirit to those who ask him! (Luke 11:13)

*Lord, teach me to be wise.*
If any of you is lacking in wisdom, ask God, who gives to all generously and ungrudgingly, and it will be given you. (James 1:5)

*Lord, take away my anxieties.*
Cast all your anxiety on [God], because he cares for you. (1 Pet. 5:7)

*Lord, help me to embrace Your moral law with every fiber of my being.*
I will put my law within them, and I will write it on their hearts; and I will be their God, and they shall be my people. (Jer. 31:33)

*Lord, if You would like me to attend daily Mass, please arrange my life so I can.*

When people come to me for spiritual direction, I ask them if they are attending daily Mass. If not, I ask them to pray this prayer and think no more about it. In almost every case, God changes their job or location or some other factor so that they can get to Mass daily. And they do it.

*Lord, make me a saint.*

> You shall be holy, for I the Lord your God am holy. (Lev. 19:2)

See also Leviticus 11:44–45 and 1 Peter 1:15–16. This is what this life is all about: becoming a saint, worthy to live in God's kingdom. Pursuing the kingdom should be our first prayer:

> Therefore do not worry, saying, "What will we eat?" or "What will we drink?" or "What will we wear?" For it is the Gentiles who strive for all these things; and indeed your heavenly Father knows that you need all these things. But strive first for the kingdom of God and his righteousness, and all these things will be given to you as well. (Matt. 6:31–33)

5

# "I'll Show Her How It Feels"

The subject of this chapter should not require much ink. Doing something malicious to an acquaintance for the purpose of showing her what is wrong with her behavior is a close cousin to revenge (doing something to get her back). And it often doesn't work.

It brings to mind a Laurel and Hardy scene where one of them gets poked by another person and he retaliates with a stronger poke. The initiator comes back with something worse, and so forth. This is how wars start. Our parents always told us, "Two wrongs don't make a right."

We have a much better chance of converting offenders by showing them *good* behavior in response to their bad — by setting a good example. St. Augustine said the three best ways to teach the Faith (and good behavior by extension) are first, by example; second, by example; and third, by example.

What's more, bearing injustices patiently is a spiritual work of mercy, as is forgiving all injuries. Showing others Christian behavior will bring about more good than showing them how their bad behavior feels.

When Jesus was on the Cross, He did not curse His executioners, or His enemies, or His parents for giving Him birth, as often happened in crucifixions. He forgave His enemies. So, although we often instinctively think we should teach the people who hurt us a lesson, that's not a good plan. Better to show them what it is like to be forgiving.

Of course, if someone is always doing you wrong, it is not wrong to be slow to see them again. You need not ask for trouble. If it could do any good, you need to tell the person why you are unhappy with his behavior. If the person gets defensive and claims he did nothing wrong, that's when you can *really* slow down the relationship. The person should know, once you have told him, just what the problem is. If the person is your co-worker or, worse yet, your boss, it might be time to consider other employment opportunities.

And, to be sure, you should refuse to hang on to residual anger. Rather, offer your hurt feelings to God as a sacrifice. As such, it can be an atonement for sin. And you will most likely have to do that over and over again. That's far better than hanging on to anger and ruining your peace.

6

# "I Can't Be Forgiven for Such a Sin Anyway, So I'll Stop Practicing the Faith"

Before we sin, God is the accuser and Satan the consoler. God says in effect, "Don't do it. You will regret it." Satan says, "Oh, don't worry, it's not so important. God will forgive you."

After we sin, God is the consoler and Satan the accuser. God says, "Come back to me. I will forgive you." Satan says, "You've done it now. You'll never stop sinning. You may as well give up."

Satan will seize upon any weakness in our thinking to keep us away from God and from communicating with Him. But we Christians have a wonderful way to recover from sin: asking pardon.

God's mercy is beyond anything we could ever imagine. He made that clear when He revealed to St. Maria Faustina, "Speak to the world about My mercy; let all mankind recognize My unfathomable mercy. While there is still time, let them have recourse to the fount of My mercy; let them profit from the Blood and Water which gushed forth for them."[41] And, "At three o'clock, implore My mercy, especially for poor sinners.... In this hour, I will refuse nothing to the soul that makes a request

[41] *Diary*, no. 848.

of Me in virtue of My Passion."[42] The gravity of the sin is no obstacle: "The greater the sinner, the greater the right he has to My mercy."[43] And even a multitude of sins is no match for God's mercy: "Encourage souls to place great trust in My fathomless mercy. Let the weak, sinful soul have no fear to approach Me, for even if it had more sins than there are grains of sand in the world, all would be drowned in the immeasurable depths of My mercy."[44]

Sin is all wrapped up in pride. Prayer for mercy is its antidote: humility. The person whose overarching desire is love will quickly get up after a serious sin, brush himself off, and continue on his journey to holiness.

Guilt is feeling bad over having intentionally sinned. Guilt is good after sinning and before confessing the sin. It is bad after confessing and receiving forgiveness in the sacrament of Penance and Reconciliation. Why? Because it is prideful to hang on to guilt after receiving absolution. In essence, it is saying, "How could someone like me have committed such a terrible sin?"

But it is *extremely* important to confess the sin and make amends. Archbishop Fulton Sheen told the story of a man who was listless, quit the company where he worked, and was unable even to motivate himself to get a new job. He had lost more than fifty pounds and looked a bit like a skeleton. His family asked Sheen to talk to him. In the course of their conversation, the man revealed that he would wipe off money whenever he gave at church. The bishop acted on that clue and asked him how much he had stolen. He replied, "I didn't steal anything." Sheen

[42] *Diary*, no. 1320.
[43] *Diary*, no. 723.
[44] *Diary*, no. 1059.

persisted and the man finally admitted that he had stolen three thousand dollars from his company. He went to Confession and then went back to his company, admitted his theft, and offered to pay it back. The company gave him back his job, and his health returned completely.[45]

 Another response to sin is doubting one's self-worth. It is the feeling that the sin has somehow completely redefined the self and made one unworthy of praying to God. This is the wrong thought that is the subject of this chapter. It often lasts for a limited time, but it paralyzes a person in spiritual matters and may even inspire him or her to commit more sins — thinking, in effect, "I'm no good, so what does it matter?"

But it *does* matter! The Enemy moves right in on such an attitude and tries to have it dominate us for as long as possible. It's like a wide receiver dropping in the end zone a pass that would have won the game. If he has any spunk, he gets up and strives to do better. This, as opposed to one who would say, "I stink; I'm going to quit this game."

We tell ourselves, "I can't believe you did that." Or, "You've made a mess now." Or, "You're a hypocrite to communicate with God after this."

The truth is, "I did that, but I will learn from that and avoid it next time." Or, "Yes, I made a mess, but life is messy. I can clean up the mess. Much of life is cleaning up messes." Or, "Communicating with God is precisely what I need now. I need to tell Him of my contrition and receive His warm embrace of forgiveness."[46]

45 *Through the Year with Fulton Sheen: Inspirational Selections for Each Day of the Year*, comp. Henry Dieterich (San Francisco: Ignatius, 2003), 188–189.
46 See similar arguments at "How to Slap Shame in the Face," Life Teen, https://lifeteen.com/blog/slap-shame-face/.

As St. John wrote, "My little children, I am writing these things to you so that you may not sin. But if anyone does sin, we have an advocate with the Father, Jesus Christ the righteous; and he is the atoning sacrifice for our sins, and not for ours only but also for the sins of the whole world" (1 John 2:1–2).

In Hebrews we read, "For we do not have a high priest who is unable to sympathize with our weaknesses, but we have one who in every respect has been tested as we are, yet without sin. Let us therefore approach the throne of grace with boldness, so that we may receive mercy and find grace to help in time of need" (Heb. 4:15–16).

The difference between Judas and Peter is that Judas saw his sin as unforgivable and committed suicide, whereas Peter sought forgiveness and found it and kept his position of primacy in the Church. He remained pope. Had Judas sought forgiveness he might be known as "St. Judas" today.

The difference between a saint and sinner is this: a saint is a sinner who never stopped trying.

7

# "I Always Commit the Same Sins;
# Why Bother Going to Confession?"

When people go to Confession to me and admit that they always confess the same sins, my response is, "So do I." One author commented on this problem as follows:

> I know it's frustrating and disappointing to think "well, here I am again." But "here I am again" doesn't have to be an admission of defeat, it could also be a prayer.
>
> Here I am again, Lord, acknowledging the necessity of you in my life. Here I am again, Lord, dependent on you. Here I am again, Lord, in need of your infinite mercy. Here I am again, Lord, in my human failings. Here I am again, Lord, thankful for your Grace.[47]

## Overcoming Habitual Sins

Once we've disposed of the sinful thought of avoiding Confession because our sins are repetitive, we can legitimately ask the

---

[47] Katrina Fernandez, "Am I a 'Catholic Failure' Because I Keep Confessing the Same Sins?" Aleteia, September 27, 2016, https:// aleteia.org/2016/09/27/am-i-a-catholic-failure-because-i-keep -confessing-the-same-sins/

question: How do we overcome habitual sins? Here is a method that has worked for me and for others as well. Write down your three major sins on an index card or a piece of paper. (It could be two or one, but never more than three.) Place it on your bureau or night table and look at it every night before retiring and again in the morning. Seeing them written should help you to be aware of them daily and to focus on striving to overcome them.

What often happens is that we really want to rid ourselves of our sins, especially our top three, but as we go about our day, we forget or lose focus on these sins. We commit them without thinking. Writing our top three sins down and seeing them in print can help us to keep those sins in mind. So, when we are faced with situations where these sins come up, we are more prepared to avoid them.

At one point, I was discussing with my sister the errors of a number of theologians. It was one of those "Isn't it awful?" sessions. As we were finishing our visit, I commented, "I guess we should be careful about being so down on these people. It could be pride on our part, even if we are right." She agreed.

The following day I put "hypercritical" at the top of my list of sins. I looked at that every day for the next year. After a year I was able to cross it off, thanks be to God.

This brings up another strategy to overcome our repeated sins: identify situations where you have most often fallen into those sins. Then devise a plan to refrain from committing them.

For example, let's say you fall into gossip repeatedly. You know that at lunchtime you and some colleagues sit and enjoy identifying the faults of your boss or of this or that fellow employee. Such fun! But sinful. So, the next time you are sitting with your fellow employees, turn the conversation to something good in the news, or something interesting you discovered. Have in mind before lunch begins what you want to bring up, and jump right in with it before the gossip begins.

## Avoiding Unchastity

Another way to stop habitual sins is to find a way to fend off the situations that lead to those sins. For example, if someone falls in using pornography often, he might put a pornography blocker on his computer or phone, or both.[48] Another way to put an end to sins against chastity is to follow the advice of Pope St. John Paul II, St. Thomas Aquinas, and Aristotle. They taught that the sexual appetite seems to have a life of its own. And, since it listens not only to reason but to the senses and imagination as well, you cannot deal with it "despotically"—that is, command it authoritatively—and expect it to obey. It won't. If you repress it in this way, it will go down into the subconscious, where it will wait for a moment of weakness and explode in a spree of sexual activity.

You must rather treat the appetite "politically"; that is, you must convince it not to go after wrong activity, by repeatedly presenting the values to be gained by chastity.[49] You must, in a sense, graft reason onto the appetite.

---

[48] One popular pornography blocker is Qustodio. It costs about $4 a month for use on up to four devices.

[49] These are some of the values you might repeat to yourself (several times a day): (1) Sex is holy, not a plaything. It should never be trivialized. (2) Created in the image of God, I can live by reason, not just by urges (as animals do). (3) Persons are to be loved, not merely used as objects of enjoyment. (4) I must not treat persons as objects, even in my mind, lest I become a user of persons in practice. (5) Unchaste activity destroys my most precious friendship, that with God, the source of all happiness. (6) Unchaste activity brings pleasure but not happiness. (7) Sexual sins tend

In other words, you must "convert the heart." Only then, when the heart is converted, does the will become free of any resentment over refusing illicit sexual activity. By repeating to oneself several times a day the benefits of chastity, you can find the peace of true chastity. Don't avoid thinking about the issue, or wait for it to come up, but daily confront your will with these values. Eventually, it will surrender to the truth.

Of course, as a fruit of the Holy Spirit, chastity requires much prayer.

## Alarms and Reminders

A further way to overcome repetitive sins is to set up an alarm to warn you when you get close to a sin. For example, if you tend to stay up too late, even though you know it will affect your mood and your performance at work the next day, program your phone to set off a warning signal when it is time to get ready for bed.

Another example is my dealing with a propensity to drive a bit too fast at times. I must have confessed this more than three hundred times, and mostly to the same confessor. I don't like to speed, but occasionally I fail to consider the speed limit and I go too fast. On occasion, the county has been kind enough to send me a photo of my car—a rather expensive one at that—to remind me to watch my speed.

At one point, I resolved to run the driving app Waze all the time, even when I know the way to my destination, to monitor

---

to drown out some of the subtle but richer loves, such as *agape* (self-giving), friendship, and affection. Adapted from Fr. Thomas G. Morrow, *Christian Dating in A Godless World* (Manchester, NH: Sophia Institute Press, 2016).

my speed. I set it up to notify me when I go five miles per hour over the speed limit and to display the speed limit at all times on my phone's GPS screen. This has worked wonders to rein in my driving excesses. Kiss the photographs goodbye!

You might also set alarms on your smartphone or your computer to remind you to pray. I have one on my computer to remind me to pray the Chaplet of Divine Mercy at three o'clock every day. An alarm might be used to remind you to pray one of the parts of the Divine Office, prayers that we priests are obliged to say daily.[50]

Reminder cards are another device for this purpose. From time to time, I forgot to pray Night Prayer. So I wrote "Night Prayer" on an index card and put it on my bed during the day. When night rolls around, I cannot miss the sign, and I remember. Speaking of signs, remembering to go to Confession periodically has been an issue for me on occasion. So I printed up some business cards that read "CONFESS!" When the time to go gets close, I leave one of these cards on the floor until I go. (I hand them out to our parishioners as well.)

## Dealing with Distractions at Prayer

Some people often mention that they have distractions during prayer. Involuntary distractions are not sins. St. John Cassian stated that it is impossible to be free from all distractions during prayer. St. Thomas Aquinas taught that involuntary distractions

---

[50] More and more laypeople are praying the Divine Office, especially since you can download an app containing these prayers on a smartphone.

do not take away the fruit of mental prayer. St. Francis de Sales wrote:

> It is not less profitable to us or less pleasing to God when [our prayer] is full of distractions; no, it will perhaps be more useful to us than if we had much consolation in it, because there will be more labor—provided, however, that we are more faithful in withdrawing from these distractions, and in refraining from dwelling upon them voluntarily.... What, then, can we do except have patience and not weary our labors, since they are undertaken for the love of God.[51]

We read in the *Catechism of the Catholic Church* (CCC):

> To set about hunting down distractions would be to fall into their trap, when all that is necessary is to turn back to our heart: for a distraction reveals to us what we are attached to, and this humble awareness before the Lord should awaken our preferential love for him and lead us resolutely to offer him our heart to be purified. Therein lies the battle, the choice of which master to serve. (2729)

The story is told of St. Bernard of Clairvaux riding on horseback with a friend when he lamented his battle with distractions during prayer. His friend commented, "I don't have any distractions at prayer." Bernard challenged him, "I will bet you this horse you cannot kneel down here and say the Our Father without being distracted."

---

[51] St. Francis de Sales, Conference 9, "On Religious Modesty," in *Spiritual Conferences*, trans. Abbot Gasquet and Canon Mackey (New York: Benziger Bros., 1909), 156.

"Okay, I'll take your bet," replied his friend. He got off his horse, knelt down and began, "Our Father who art in heaven." He stopped, looked up, and asked, "Do I get the saddle, too?"

## Bad Language

Another sin that is often confessed is cursing or using foul language. One way to end that habit is to say a short prayer as a penance right after you say a bad word. You'll get so tired of saying those prayers that you'll reform.

We could use the same tactic to correct impolite language. If we fail to say please or thank you, we say a prayer. Incidentally, being polite with children is a great way to teach them courtesy.

∾

The important thing is not that we completely overcome all of our sins but that we never stop trying to do so. Discouragement over failing to stop bad habits is natural; it is worse when we minimize the damage done by those sins and let temptation have its way.

8

# "Go Ahead, It's Only A Venial Sin"

Saying, "Go ahead, it's only a venial sin" is like saying, "I will smack my wife just once. She won't be scarred by it." Committing even a venial sin against God is, as all the saints knew, an awful thing. And it hurts us a great deal.

St. Ignatius of Loyola avowed that he would not, "for the sake of all creation, or for the purpose of saving my life, consider committing a single venial sin."[52] St. Catherine of Genoa wrote:

> When I beheld that vision in which I saw the magnitude of the stain of even one least sin against God, I know not why I did not die. I said: "I no longer marvel that Hell is so horrible, since it was made for sin; for even Hell (as I have seen it) I do not believe to be really proportionate to the dreadfulness of sin; on the contrary, it seems to me that even in Hell God is very merciful, since I have beheld the terrible stain caused by but one venial sin."[53]

[52] St. Ignatius of Loyola, *Spiritual Exercises*, trans. Anthony Mottola (Garden City, NY: Image Books, 1964), 2nd week, 12th day, 82.

[53] St. Catherine of Genoa, *The Life and Doctrine of Saint Catherine of Genoa* (New York: Christian Press Association, 1907), chap. 22, http://www.ccel.org/ccel/catherine_g/life.html.

The saints' great love for God made them keenly aware of the damage done by even venial sins. St. Francis of Assisi said, "Even though I had committed but one little sin I would have ample reason to repent of it for the rest of my life."[54] In her diary, St. Maria Faustina wrote of a locution that came during a Forty Hours' devotion: "The Lord said to me, My daughter, write that involuntary offenses of souls do not hinder My love for them or prevent Me from uniting Myself with them. But voluntary offenses, even the smallest, obstruct My graces, and I cannot lavish My gifts on such souls."[55]

St. John Henry Newman claimed that "the Church holds it better for sun and moon to drop from Heaven, for the earth to fail, and for all the many millions on it to die of starvation in the most extreme agony as far as temporal affliction goes, than that one soul, I will not say, should be lost, but should commit one single venial sin, should tell one willful untruth or should steal one poor farthing without excuse."[56]

What is so terrible about sin? Why the fuss? Because we are called to an intimate life of love with God, a kind of marriage (see Ezek. 16; Isa. 52; Hos. 1–3). If we are to be in this marriage, we must be holy, and every act that brings us away from that goal is a terrible tragedy.

Jesus told us what we must do to enter the Kingdom:

A lawyer stood up to test Jesus. "Teacher," he said, "what must I do to inherit eternal life?" He said to him, "What

---

[54] Quoted at MyCatholicSource.com, http://www.mycatholic-source.com/mcs/qt/saint_francis_reflections_teachings.htm.

[55] *Diary*, no. 1641.

[56] John Henry (Cardinal) Newman, *Apologia pro Vita Sua* (New York: E. P. Dutton, 1955), 354–355.

is written in the law? What do you read there?" He answered, "You shall love the Lord your God with all your heart, and with all your soul, and with all your strength, and with all your mind; and your neighbor as yourself." And he said to him, "You have given the right answer; do this, and you will live." (Luke 10:25–28)

What if we appear before the Lord on Judgment Day with venial sins we have not atoned for? Not good. We would spend time in purgatory. The *Catechism of the Catholic Church* teaches:

> The Church gives the name Purgatory to this final purification of the elect, which is entirely different from the punishment of the damned.[57] The Church formulated her doctrine of faith on Purgatory especially at the Councils of Florence and Trent. The tradition of the Church, by reference to certain texts of Scripture, speaks of a cleansing fire: "As for certain lesser faults, we must believe that, before the Final Judgment, there is a purifying fire (cf. 1 Cor. 3:15; 1 Pet. 1:7)." (1031)

Pope Paul VI taught that it is a truth "divinely revealed that sins bring punishments inflicted by God's sanctity and justice. These must be expiated either on this earth through the sorrows, miseries and calamities of this life, and above all, through death, or else in the life beyond, through fire and torments or 'purifying' punishments."[58]

---

[57] Cf. Council of Florence (1439): DS 1304; Council of Trent (1563): DS 1820; (1547):1580; see also Benedict XII, *Benedictus Deus* (1336): DS 1000.

[58] Pope Paul VI, Apostolic Constitution *Indulgentiarum Doctrina* (On the Revision of Indulgences) (January 1, 1967), no. 2.

How difficult is purgatory? St. Thomas Aquinas taught, "In purgatory there will be a twofold loss, namely the delay of the divine vision, and the pain of sense, namely the punishment by bodily fire. With regard to both, the least pain of Purgatory surpasses the greatest pain of this life."[59]

So purgatory is no picnic.[60] Venial sins harm our relationship with God. They bring sorrows and miseries in this life, and, worse yet, they entail the torments of purgatory. With this in mind, could we ever say, "It's only a venial sin"?

---

[59] St. Thomas Aquinas, *Summa Theologiae*, appendix 1, q. 2, art. 1.
[60] For more on purgatory, see my book *Be Holy: A Catholic's Guide to the Spiritual Life* (Cincinnati: Servant, 2009) or my booklet *God's Wake Up Call: Heaven, Purgatory & Hell*, https://cfalive.com/collections/booklets/products/gods-wake-up-call-heaven-Purgatory-Hell.

9

# "I Don't Feel Forgiven, So I Guess I'm Not"

Occasionally people will want to reconfess a serious sin such as abortion many years after having confessed it the first time, saying "I don't feel forgiven." The truth is that if it was confessed with true contrition it *was* forgiven. What such people may be feeling is that they haven't *made up* for the sin. The penances given in Confession are not designed to totally make up for the sins confessed.

In the fourth and fifth centuries they were. The penance for one of the three major sins of murder, adultery or fornication, or denying the Faith was truly severe. You might have to spend ten or fifteen years in penance for one instance of these, and if you were married, you could never again have relations with your spouse. If you were not married, you could never *get* married.

Needless to say, people guilty of these things were not coming in great numbers to go to Confession. They would put off going to Confession as long as possible, usually until their deathbeds.

It appears that the Church noted this and began to ease up on the penances. It seems it was deemed best to get people forgiven as soon as possible, to prevent them from losing their souls, even if the penances had to be reduced considerably. The penances became more symbolic, *representing* rather than actually matching all that might be needed to make up for the sins confessed.

This is why we are encouraged to do penance every Friday and throughout the season of Lent. At those times, we share in the redemptive mission of Christ by doing penance for our sins and the sins of the world.

## Methods of Penance

Perhaps the most common way of doing penance is to fast from food on Fridays (and perhaps Wednesdays as well) until sundown. When I fast, I usually skip breakfast and take something small for lunch, such as bread and water or an apple. Then I eat a normal dinner. This is not hard-core fasting, but it is worth something.

Fasting applies not only to food but also to other enjoyable things, such as listening to music or watching television. I fast from all sports news on Wednesdays and Fridays. That is harder for me than giving up food. Watching television can be an addictive drug for some. When I got ordained, I resolved to abstain from TV every day except Sundays and feast days. That's one of the best decisions I ever made.

Fasting and doing penance are primarily about denying the will, not just the body. The Lord said to St. Catherine of Siena, "He who desires for My sake to mortify his body with many penances, and not his own will, did not give Me much pleasure."[61] And, of course, fasting or doing penance must always be done with prudence. Fasting to the point of ruining your health is not pleasing to God, as St. Bernard learned the hard way.

Is fasting an *option* for Christians, or is it an *obligation*? Well, what did our blessed Lord say about it? We read in Mark:

[61] *Dialogue of St. Catherine of Siena*, 55.

Now John's disciples and the Pharisees were fasting; and people came and said to him, "Why do John's disciples and the disciples of the Pharisees fast, but your disciples do not fast?" Jesus said to them, "The wedding guests cannot fast while the bridegroom is with them, can they? As long as they have the bridegroom with them, they cannot fast. The days will come when the bridegroom is taken away from them, and then they will fast on that day." (Mark 2:18–20)

Notice that our Lord did not say that His disciples *might* fast after He had gone; He said that they *will* fast. St. Thomas Aquinas wrote that "fasting is useful as atoning for and preventing sin, and as raising the mind to spiritual things; and everyone is bound by the natural dictate of reason to practice fasting as far as it is necessary for these purposes."[62]

So, St. Thomas believed that fasting is required by our human nature. According to canon law, all Christians are obliged to fast:

All members of the Christian faithful in their own way are bound to do penance in virtue of divine law; in order that all may be joined in a common observance of penance, penitential days are prescribed in which the Christian faithful in a special way pray, exercise works of piety and charity, and deny themselves by fulfilling their responsibilities more faithfully and especially by observing fast and abstinence according to the norm of the following canons.[63]

The following canons (1250–1253) specify the laws of fasting and abstinence. The Church prescribes two days for fasting: Ash

---

[62] St. Thomas Aquinas, *Summa Theologiae*, II-II, q. 147, art. 3.
[63] *Code of Canon Law*, no. 1249.

Wednesday and Good Friday. On those days, people over eighteen and under fifty-nine have an obligation to eat only one full meal. Two other meals may be eaten, but taken together they must be equivalent to less than the one normal-size meal.

What if you are sick on a fast day, and you need to eat? Then you should eat. Prudence should govern fasting.

In addition to the two fast days, the Church prescribes Ash Wednesday and the Fridays of Lent as days of abstinence from meat for those fourteen or older. Is that all the fasting we should do? It depends on the person, but most of us should do other fasting as well.

How do you know when your fasting is reasonable? It should make you uncomfortable but should not interfere with the carrying out of your duties. Incidentally, this question as to how to be sure your fasting is reasonable is precisely why the spiritual greats of the Church have always recommended that you fast under the direction of a spiritual director.

Your fasting should not make others uncomfortable. If someone invites you out to dinner on a Friday when you've been fasting all day, do not just sit there with two pieces of bread and some water at your place; eat a small portion of the normal meal with everyone else. Remember, fasting is the denial of the will, not just of the body.

∞

Because penance helps atone for sin, it can make us feel more strongly that our sins are forgiven. But the key point is that forgiveness is not dependent on our feelings. If we have asked forgiveness—normally expressed through the sacrament of Confession—then we can have assurance that God has forgiven us. Wallowing in the guilt of past sins is itself a sinful thought. We are called instead to rejoice in God's mercy.

10

# "I Don't Believe Everything I Read in the Gospel or in Church Teaching"

Let's tackle the Gospel first. Citing the Second Vatican Council's Constitution on Divine Revelation, the *Catechism of the Catholic Church* asserts: "The inspired books teach the truth. 'Since therefore all that the inspired authors or sacred writers affirm should be regarded as affirmed by the Holy Spirit, we must acknowledge that the books of Scripture firmly, faithfully, and without error teach that truth which God, for the sake of our salvation, wished to see confided to the Sacred Scriptures'" (107; *Dei Verbum* 11).

That being stated, there are several senses in which the Scriptures can be understood: the literal, the allegorical, the moral, and the anagogical. The literal sense is the plain sense — for example the description of Jesus' raising Lazarus from the dead, or Jesus' dying and rising from the dead. The allegorical sense is that in which there is a veiled or hidden meaning to what is stated. St. Paul speaks of the two sons of Abraham being an allegory. The first son was born of the slave woman. She symbolized the first covenant, that of the law. The other mother, the free woman, represents the Jerusalem above, the new Jerusalem, our mother (Gal. 4:21ff.).

Many of the Old Testament occurrences have been seen as "types" of New Testament realities. For example, the escape of the Israelites through the Red Sea is seen as a foreshadowing, a type of Baptism. Isaac's carrying the wood for his sacrifice is seen as a foreshadowing of Jesus' carrying His Cross. And Solomon and his kingdom of peace are seen as a foreshadowing of Jesus, the Son of David, ushering in the Kingdom of everlasting peace. All of these fall under the theme of allegory.

The moral sense of Scripture concerns how God wants us to behave. Examples of this include the Ten Commandments, the teaching of Jesus on divorce and remarriage (Luke 16:18), and the teaching of Jesus on fornication, murder, and theft (Mark 7:21–23).

The anagogical sense has to do with the eternal implications of how we live our lives, especially regarding our salvation. Examples are the parable of the sheep and goats (Matt. 25:31–46) and the condition for following Jesus—the cross. "If any want to become my followers, let them deny themselves and take up their cross and follow me. For those who want to save their life will lose it, and those who lose their life for my sake will find it" (Matt. 16:24–25).

Of course, there is need for interpretation of Sacred Scripture. Our separated brethren of other Christian churches suggest that each person is to interpret the Scriptures himself. The Catholic Church, in contrast, provides her adherents a unified interpretation of Sacred Scripture: "According to a saying of the Fathers, Sacred Scripture is written principally in the Church's heart rather than in documents and records, for the Church carries in her Tradition the living memorial of God's Word, and it is the Holy Spirit who gives her the spiritual interpretation of the Scripture."[64]

[64] CCC, no. 113.

So it is very important that we accept all the teaching found in Sacred Scripture as interpreted by the Church. St. Augustine wrote, "If you believe what you like in the Gospel, and reject what you don't like, it is not the Gospel you believe, but yourself."

## Church Teaching on Morality

What about the Church's moral teaching? The Second Vatican Council's Dogmatic Constitution on the Church explains:

> Although the individual bishops do not enjoy the prerogative of infallibility, they nevertheless proclaim Christ's doctrine infallibly whenever, even though dispersed through the world, but still maintaining the bond of communion among themselves and with the successor of Peter, and authentically teaching matters of faith and morals, they are in agreement on one position as definitively to be held.[65]

Pope St. John Paul II commented on the reality of dissent from moral teachings in a 1987 speech in the United States:

> It is sometimes reported that a large number of Catholics today do not adhere to the teachings of the Church on a number of questions, notably sexual and conjugal morality, divorce and remarriage. Some are reported as not accepting the Church's clear position on abortion. It has also been noted that there is a tendency on the part of some Catholics to be selective in their adherence to the Church's moral teachings. It is sometimes claimed that

---

[65] Second Vatican Council, Dogmatic Constitution on the Church *Lumen Gentium* (November 21, 1964), no. 25.

dissent from the *Magisterium* is totally compatible with being a "good Catholic" and poses no obstacle to the reception of the sacraments. This is a grave error.[66]

Being unable to receive the sacraments means one is not in the state of grace, but is in the state of mortal sin. Remaining in a state of mortal sin has serious implications regarding a person's candidacy for salvation.

What are the moral teachings the Holy Father was referring to? The teaching on divorce and remarriage comes from Christ Himself: "Anyone who divorces his wife and marries another commits adultery" (Luke 16:18). The teaching on fornication is also from Jesus: "For it is from within, from the human heart, that evil intentions come: fornication, theft, murder.... All these evil things come from within, and they defile a person" (Mark 7:21, 23). The immorality of adultery is from the Ten Commandments and is reiterated by Jesus in Mark 10:19. The Church teaching on abortion is based on the Fifth Commandment and is clearly spelled out in St. John Paul II's encyclical *Evangelium Vitae*: "I declare that direct abortion, that is, abortion willed as an end or as a means, always constitutes a grave moral disorder, since it is the deliberate killing of an innocent human being."[67]

What about the teaching on contraception? In 1997, the Vatican's Pontifical Council for the Family stated:

> The Church has always taught the intrinsic evil of con-traception, that is, of every marital act intentionally

---

[66] Address of His Holiness John Paul II, meeting with the bishops of the United States, Los Angeles (September 16, 1987).

[67] Pope John Paul II, Encyclical Letter *Evangelium Vitae* (*The Gospel of Life*) (March 25, 1995), no. 62.

rendered unfruitful. This teaching is to be held as definitive and irreformable. Contraception is gravely opposed to marital chastity; it is contrary to the good of the transmission of life (the procreative aspect of matrimony), and to the reciprocal self-giving of the spouses (the unitive aspect of matrimony); it harms true love and denies the sovereign role of God in the transmission of human life.[68]

Did Jesus intend the Church to teach about moral issues even if not explicitly covered in Scripture? It seems so. In Luke 10:16, He told those whom He sent, "Whoever listens to you listens to me." He also told the apostles, "I am with you always, to the end of the age" (Matt. 28:20). Did He mean that He would be there encouraging the Church, sitting by while it taught errors on the moral life?

When He knocked Paul to the ground for persecuting the Church, did Jesus say, "Saul, Saul, why are you persecuting my Church?" No, He said, "Why are you persecuting *me?*" Jesus identifies with His Church.

So it is of great importance that we embrace Church teachings that are taught definitively and authoritatively, such as those mentioned above.

---

[68] Pontifical Council for the Family, *Vademecum for Confessors concerning Some Aspects of the Morality of the Conjugal Life* (February 12, 1997), chap. 2, no. 4.

11

# "I Don't Have to Help the Poor Because They Don't Help Themselves"

From one of my former parishioners:

> I can still remember the day my husband and I decided to start tithing. We were living in a very small basement apartment of a friend's house. We moved there because our previous landlord was raising our rent every year by the hundreds and we knew that the money would be better spent on a mortgage. We had wanted a house close to St. Bernadette's because it had been our parish for several years, but it was proving to be impossible. The market at the time was fast. Homes were being listed and sold within a week and our price range didn't help. We had been house hunting for eight months and the only homes we could afford were foreclosed, dilapidated houses. We came back from seeing one of them, and I was in tears.
>
> That's when my husband said something radical: "Honey, I think we need to start tithing." Needless to say, I wasn't very charitable—what an insane idea! We lived on a single income, had bills, debt, and now we were going to give what little we had and more to God?! God knew

our financial problems and obligations and He certainly didn't need our 10 percent!

"You're right. He doesn't, but we're in need of His grace and maybe this will help," my husband said. I thought about it, prayed about it and after a few days of more frustrating house hunting we surrendered to God and started tithing.

Three months had passed and with it came bills, car repairs, and more dilapidated homes to see. Still, the first check we wrote when we did our budget was to God and there was always enough to put food on the table and pay for the essentials. Then one morning, I got an e-mail for a listing of a four-bedroom, three-bath home in our price range. I called my agent, and we went to see it that morning. My mouth dropped because I couldn't believe how everything about this home was what I always wanted and it was listed at a low price! Best of all, it was only five minutes from St. Bernadette's! We immediately signed the contract and started praying.

Bidding wars were typical, and we found out that afternoon that three other contracts were offered to the owners. The next day our realtor called and told us they accepted our contract! That was one of the many miracles of our home. Because the realtor was not from the area, she underpriced the house by $30,000. The other contracts offered more money, but the owners wanted ours because we were the first ones to see it. And to make sure we knew that this was a sign from God, the day our contract was accepted was on the feast day of St. Bernadette.

Eight years have passed since we started tithing, and God has outdone us in generosity. My husband's job brought him several promotions, and now he is a Unit

Chief in the government. Our children are blessed to go to amazing Catholic schools because of the generosity of grants from their schools. Not only do we have food on the table and a roof over our heads: God provides more than enough for us and is more generous to us than we were to ourselves eight years ago.

Yes, the temptations come to give less, but looking back at where we were and where God has brought us, there is no doubt in our hearts and minds that the first check we write will always be to Him. Another miracle that tithing has given our family is freedom. Realizing that all belongs to God and that we are stewards meant to do His will gives us a great sense of peace. We understand now that God cannot give you grace unless you open the door for Him. Tithing is about trust — trusting that God can never be outdone in generosity, trusting that He will take care of you and your needs, but most of all trusting in His will and that His will is Love.

That generous family has been giving to their parish and a number of charities for more than fifteen years. They have lived out the message in Proverbs: "Some give freely, yet grow all the richer; others withhold what is due, and only suffer want. A generous person will be enriched, and one who gives water will get water" (Prov. 11:24–25).

Helping the poor is not an option for the Christian. In Matthew 25, Jesus made it clear that helping the poor is absolutely necessary:

> He will put the sheep at his right hand and the goats at the left. Then the king will say to those at his right hand, "Come, you that are blessed by my Father, inherit

the kingdom prepared for you from the foundation of the world; for I was hungry and you gave me food, I was thirsty and you gave me something to drink, I was a stranger and you welcomed me, I was naked and you gave me clothing, I was sick and you took care of me, I was in prison and you visited me." Then the righteous will answer him, "Lord, when was it that we saw you hungry and gave you food, or thirsty and gave you something to drink? And when was it that we saw you a stranger and welcomed you, or naked and gave you clothing? And when was it that we saw you sick or in prison and visited you?" And the king will answer them, "Truly I tell you, just as you did it to one of the least of these who are members of my family, you did it to me." Then he will say to those at his left hand, "You that are accursed, depart from me into the eternal fire prepared for the devil and his angels; for I was hungry and you gave me no food, I was thirsty and you gave me nothing to drink, I was a stranger and you did not welcome me, naked and you did not give me clothing, sick and in prison and you did not visit me." Then they also will answer, "Lord, when was it that we saw you hungry or thirsty or a stranger or naked or sick or in prison, and did not take care of you?" Then he will answer them, "Truly I tell you, just as you did not do it to one of the least of these, you did not do it to me." (Matt. 25:33–45)

It is hard to imagine a stronger statement by Jesus on the need to help the poor.

Also, in Luke 16:19–24, we find Jesus saying,

There was a rich man who was dressed in purple and fine linen and who feasted sumptuously every day. And at his gate lay a poor man named Lazarus, covered with sores, who longed to satisfy his hunger with what fell from the rich man's table; even the dogs would come and lick his sores. The poor man died and was carried away by the angels to be with Abraham. The rich man also died and was buried. In Hades, where he was being tormented, he looked up and saw Abraham far away with Lazarus by his side. He called out, "Father Abraham, have mercy on me, and send Lazarus to dip the tip of his finger in water and cool my tongue; for I am in agony in these flames."

It seems clear that the rich man ended in hell! There are only two places in Sacred Scripture where people are sent to hell. Here, in the parable of Lazarus and the rich man, and in Matthew 25, in the parable of the sheep and the goats. In both cases, the condemned were those who did not help the poor. Jesus confirms this: "None of you can become my disciple if you do not give up all your possessions" (Luke 14:33).

St. John adds to the evidence that we must help the poor: "How does God's love abide in anyone who has the world's goods and sees a brother or sister in need and yet refuses help? Little children, let us love, not in word or speech, but in truth and action" (1 John 3:17–18).

St. Ambrose had strong words about helping the poor: "You are not making a gift of your possessions to the poor person. You are handing over to him what is his. For, what has been given in common for the use of all, you have claimed for yourself. The world is given to all, and not only to the rich."[69]

---

[69] As quoted in Pope Paul VI, Encyclical Letter *Populorum Progressio* (On the Development of Peoples) (March 26, 1967), no. 23, n. 22.

In other words, we are in some way responsible for the continuing poverty of others in our world. We are "our brother's keeper."[70] The penalty for not helping those in need is eternal punishment, as we saw in Matthew 25.

What about the argument that the poor don't help themselves? There are some who take advantage of charity, and we should avoid enabling laziness where it is obvious (see 2 Thess. 3). But so many of the world's poor are not to blame for their plight. Consider those made poor by hurricanes, as occurred in Puerto Rico (Maria, 2017), Florida (Michael, 2018), and Haiti (Matthew, 2016). What about the Indian Ocean tsunami (2004), which killed more than two hundred thousand people and caused widespread devastation?

What are some of the greatest causes of poverty worldwide? They include:
1. Lack of access to clean water and nutritious food
2. Lack of available jobs
3. Armed conflicts: in some countries, such as Syria, large numbers of refugees were forced to leave behind homes and possessions due to conflicts and are now in serious poverty.
4. Lack of educational opportunities[71]

As this shows, it is not laziness that causes most poverty.

---

[70] "Am I my brother's keeper?" was the reply of Cain, after he had killed his brother, when the Lord asked, "Where is your brother?" (Gen. 4:9). This impertinent answer from a murderer is clearly unacceptable.

[71] "11 Top Causes of Global Poverty," Concern Worldwide US, March 2020, https://www.concernusa.org/story/top-9-causes -global-poverty/.

Scripture proclaims how praiseworthy it is to give alms (do-nations to the poor): "Store up almsgiving in your treasury, and it will rescue you from every disaster" (Sir. 29:12). "As water extinguishes a blazing fire, so almsgiving atones for sin" (Sir. 3:30). How God loves almsgiving!

Are there certain charities known for being most helpful to the poor and for promoting the Faith? Yes, the following are recommended: Catholic Near East Welfare Association, Aid to the Church in Need, Society for the Propagation of the Faith, and Knights of Columbus Disaster Relief.

Should every Christian live some degree of poverty so as to be able to help the poor? Yes! In his excellent book *Happy Are You Poor*, Thomas Dubay states, "Scripture scholars seem to be of one mind (I have come across no one of another mind) that most New Testament texts that deal with poverty as an ideal are meant to be applied to all who follow Christ."[72]

The Lord is hard on the rich. "Woe to you who are rich, for you have received your consolation" (Luke 6:24). "Truly I tell you, it will be hard for a rich person to enter the kingdom of heaven. Again I tell you, it is easier for a camel to go through the eye of a needle than for someone who is rich to enter the kingdom of God" (Matt. 19:23–24). That is hyperbole, but it is still pretty strong. So strong that it disturbed the disciples, prompting Jesus to say that for men it is impossible, but for God all things are possible.

And we read in St. James, "For the sun rises with its scorching heat and withers the field; its flower falls, and its beauty perishes.

---

[72] Thomas Dubay, *Happy Are You Poor* (San Francisco: Ignatius Press, 2003), 13.

# Overcoming Sinful Thoughts

It is the same way with the rich; in the midst of a busy life, they will wither away" (James 1:11). And from St. Paul,

> Of course, there is great gain in godliness combined with contentment; for we brought nothing into the world, so that we can take nothing out of it; but if we have food and clothing, we will be content with these. But those who want to be rich fall into temptation and are trapped by many senseless and harmful desires that plunge people into ruin and destruction. For the love of money is a root of all kinds of evil, and in their eagerness to be rich some have wandered away from the faith and pierced themselves with many pains. (1 Tim. 6:6–10)

Why is Jesus so hard on the rich? St. Ignatius of Loyola wrote in the *Spiritual Exercises*: "[The devil] bids [his demons] first to tempt men with the lust of riches ... that they may thereby more easily gain the empty honor of the world, and then come to unbounded pride. The first step in his snare is that of riches, the second honor, and the third, pride."[73] Pride is the root of every vice.

"Well, I'm not really rich," some will say. "I live comfortably, but I'm not rich." But, if we look at world history, we in the United States are some of the richest people who have ever lived. And if we look at other parts of the world—Africa, India, South and Central America—we could hardly be seen as anything but rich. As of the early part of the twenty-first century, the "first world" (the United States, Canada, Australia, New Zealand, and Western and Northern Europe) had a gross national product per

---

[73] Ignatius of Loyola, *Spiritual Exercises* (Garden City, NY: Doubleday, 1964), 76.

capita of roughly three times that of the "second world" (including Russia, Eastern Europe, and China); about five or six times that of "third world" countries (including parts of Africa and Latin America); and more than twenty times that of "fourth world" countries (including central and lower African countries such as Chad, Ethiopia, Mali, Togo, and Zambia; Asian countries such as Afghanistan, Bangladesh, and Cambodia; and Samoa, the Solomon Islands, and Haiti).[74]

St. John Paul II said in 1979 at Yankee Stadium, "You must never be content to leave [the poor] the crumbs from your feast. You must take of your substance and not just your abundance to help them. And, you must treat them like guests at your family table."[75]

How can a rich person live some degree of poverty? By being so generous with the poor that he *must* live simply. We read in Luke, "Sell your possessions, and give alms. Make purses for yourselves that do not wear out, an unfailing treasure in heaven, where no thief comes near and no moth destroys. For where your treasure is, there your heart will be also" (Luke 12:33–34).

Some of the poorest of the poor are children in the womb. We certainly can't say *they* don't help themselves! Donating time and money to pro-life groups is a wonderful way to help the poor. St. John Paul II wrote in 1994:

> According to the Gospel of Matthew the Final Judgment will contain another list, solemn and terrifying: "Depart from me ... for I was hungry and you gave me no food, I was thirsty and you gave me no drink, I was a stranger

[74] Dubay, *Blessed Are You Poor*, 63.
[75] Pope John Paul II, Homily at Yankee Stadium (October 2, 1979).

and you did not welcome me, naked and you did not clothe me" (Matt. 25:41–43). To this list also we could add other ways of acting, in which Jesus is present in each case as the "one who has been rejected." In this way he would identify with the abandoned wife or husband, or with the child conceived and then rejected "You did not welcome me"![76]

To say we won't help the poor because they don't help themselves is wrong on two counts. First, many of the poor haven't the tools, without our help, to help themselves. And secondly, helping the poor is an absolute necessity for the Christian. It is one of the conditions for being saved.

---

[76] John Paul II, *Letter to Families* (February 2, 1994), no. 22.

12

# "Go Ahead! Everyone Is Doing It"

"Grandpa, everyone is doing it." This could have been a response from any young person — or anyone — regarding stealing music recordings on the Internet some years ago. But a Christian who has thought about the virtue of justice and our need to practice it would never accept such behavior. It is stealing: stealing a product provided by a musician for which he deserved a payment. When we meet the Lord, He won't ask how many people were doing it.

This same argument might be put forth for the practice of premarital sex. It seems to be true that many people are "doing it." However, it is also true that the divorce rate is higher for those who sleep together before marriage.[77] Of course, the benefit of

---

[77] For example, a 2018 article in the *Atlantic* quotes W. Bradford Wilcox, a sociologist and senior fellow at the Institute for Family Studies: "Contrary to conventional wisdom, when it comes to sex, less experience is better, at least for the marriage." Another sociologist found that, "by the 2010s ... just 5 percent of new brides were virgins. And just 6 percent of their marriages dissolved within five years, compared with 20 percent for most people." Olga Khazan, "Fewer Sex Partners Means a Happier Marriage," *Atlantic*, October 22, 2018, https://www.theatlantic.com/health/archive/2018/10/sexual -partners-and-marital-happiness/573493/.

having a good marriage is in addition to that of being able to live in the state of grace and have the blessings that come with that.

Being among the majority has not historically been a sure indication of being right. How many Southerners were in favor of slavery in 1860? How many in England favored it before Wilberforce raised consciences in Parliament and it was outlawed? How many in Nazi Germany paid little attention to the genocidal atrocities of Adolf Hitler?

Human beings tend to follow the crowd, and that is not always bad. "There is a heuristic most of us use to determine what to do, think, say, and buy: the principle of social proof. To learn what is correct, we look at what other people are doing. In his bestselling book *Influence: The Psychology of Persuasion*, psychologist Robert Cialdini writes, 'Whether the question is what to do with an empty popcorn box in a movie theater, how fast to drive on a certain stretch of highway, or how to eat the chicken at a dinner party, the actions of those around us will be important in defining the answer.' Social proof is a shortcut to deciding how to act."[78]

Cialdini applied the crowd-following principle to reduce the stealing of wood in Arizona's Petrified Forest National Park. Visitors at the park were greeted with signs stating, "Your heritage is being vandalized every day by theft losses of petrified wood of 14 tons a year, mostly a small piece at a time." Cialdini had the signs removed from one path in the park to see if it made a difference. It did. The path without the sign had one-third less wood stolen than the paths with the sign. Apparently, the placard

---

[78] Quoted in Rob Henderson, "The Science behind Why People Follow the Crowd" *Psychology Today*, May 24, 2017, https://www. psychologytoday.com/us/blog/after-service/201705/the-science -behind-why-people-follow-the-crowd.

signaled visitors that taking pieces of wood was normal since so many had been doing it.

Admittedly, there can be benefits to following the crowd. If a book on a subject we are interested in is on the best-seller list, we would probably enjoy reading it. If an item is ranked in the top five in sales among different brands of a product, it's probably pretty good.

Cialdini points out that most of us haven't the time to learn in advance about things we buy, so we depend on popularity, and it usually works. Of course, now with the Internet, it is much easier to check on quality before we buy. If an item has received a five-star rating from hundreds of people, it is even more likely to be good than if it is merely popular. A rating of excellence is worth more than popularity.

Our subject at hand, however, is not the goodness of a product but the goodness of a behavior. That is much more critical inasmuch as it bears on our relationship with God, and our salvation. To determine good behavior, we need a reference point, and that is the Word of God and the teaching of the Church Jesus founded. Jesus is only too happy to tell us what behavior is good and what behavior is not, because He wants us to be happy. Bad behavior never brings true happiness; good behavior does.

Returning to our original example, stealing copyrighted materials may seem easy and good, but in stealing we fail in justice. Justice is one of the cardinal virtues, and is one of many virtues by which we will be judged. (We need *all* the virtues to enter the Kingdom of God.)

Regarding the example of premarital sex, Jesus addressed this in Sacred Scripture: "It is from within, from the human heart, that evil intentions come: fornication, theft, murder, adultery, avarice, wickedness, deceit, licentiousness, envy, slander, pride, folly. All these evil things come from within, and they defile a person" (Mark 7:21–23).

So, while popularity might be of use for us to choose a book or another item, it often will not help us to determine what is good behavior. William Penn put it well: "Wrong is wrong even if everyone is doing it; right is right even if no one is doing it." We should keep in mind the words of our Lord: "The gate is wide and the road is easy that leads to destruction, and there are many who take it. For the gate is narrow and the road is hard that leads to [eternal] life, and there are few who find it" (Matt. 7:13–14).

# 13

# "Since I Already Committed a Mortal Sin, I May as Well Commit Some More"

This wrongheaded thought is an example of legalistic solipsism, a concern for the self without reference to others—namely, God. It is like saying, "I have committed adultery with one woman and must confess that to my wife. I may as well commit adultery with several more women so I can confess to my wife several infidelities at once." This is a thought straight from hell—and it leads to hell.

A person who loves God will feel remorse if he commits a mortal sin and will express his sorrow right after the sin by making a sincere act of contrition and resolving to get to Confession as soon as possible. The whole economy of sin and forgiveness in the Church is to strive always for perfection and to be in close friendship with God at all times. "Be perfect ... as your heavenly Father is perfect" (Matt. 5:48).

The person who truly desires to love God wants to be close to God at every moment. If he falls, he gets back up right away and returns to his merciful Father. God is merciful, but He is not an enabler. He forgives those who are truly sorry and who are willing to reform.

Is it possible that, knowing God's unfathomable mercy, a sinner might try to take advantage of it? Yes, of course, but that's

the risk God is willing to take to give us confidence in His unfailing love.

St. John Henry Newman showed insight when he wrote of
the Old Testament figure Balaam, "His endeavor was, not to
please God, but to please self without displeasing God."[79] If you
love God, you will not accumulate many sins so as to confess
them all at one time.

The person who takes the attitude that being in the state of
mortal sin is a license to commit more such sins assumes that sin
makes one happy. Not so. The moral law is the manufacturer's
operating specifications. It is the way to fulfillment and happiness. The witnesses to that truth are the saints. They were all
quite happy doing the will of God.

This, incidentally, is why canon law insists that penitents
confess mortal sins by type and (approximate) number.[80] Adding to our sins should add to our guilt, and it certainly adds to
our misery.

One benefit of confessing the number of mortal sins committed is that it helps people to be aware that they are sinful only in
particular ways and not in general. Catholic anthropology holds
that people are fundamentally good and only wounded by sin.
This stands in opposition to the idea, held by other theological

[79] "Obedience without Love, as Instanced in the Character of
Balaam," Sermon 2 in *Parochial and Plain Sermons*, vol. 4, *Newman Reader*, http://newmanreader.org/works/parochial/volume4/
sermon2.html.

[80] Canon 988.1 states: "A member of the Christian faithful is
obliged to confess in kind and number all grave sins committed
after baptism and not yet remitted directly through the keys
of the Church nor acknowledged in individual confession, [of
which the person has knowledge after diligent examination of
conscience]."

traditions, that human beings are totally corrupted by sin and can only hope for grace to cover over that sin.

It is a lot worse to intentionally get drunk ten times than just once. Anyone who is concerned about loving God and seeking his or her own happiness should know that. The best course of action for someone who has just committed a mortal sin is to say an Act of Contrition out of love and plan on getting to Confession as soon as possible — and of course, that person should get back to prayer right away.

14

# "I Can't Control My Feelings;
That's Just Who I Am"

"I can't control my feelings; that's just who I am." The first part of this statement is true. The second is not. We are not defined by our feelings; we are defined by what we *do* with our feelings. People often tell me that their sins include anger they feel about someone or something. Angry feelings are not intrinsically sinful. What is sinful is to act on them in unreasonable, sinful, ways. But it is also somewhat sinful to dwell on that anger and let it dominate our hearts and minds, or to let it take up a lot of space in our minds, even if we don't act on it irrationally.

We should acknowledge our anger to ourselves and identify why we are angry. Next, we should decide whether it is worth worrying about. Perhaps we will say to ourselves, "That's not a big deal. Just forget it." If it is a big deal and we judge that it could do some good, we should try to speak to the person who angered us to correct the situation.[81] If trying to correct it would just make things worse (as in trying to correct a narcissistic boss), then we have to bring it to God. We should offer it to God as a

---

[81] If we correct others for every discomfort, it may be too much. We should pick our battles.

sacrifice for sin and keep offering it each time it comes up in our minds. And then we should refuse to think about it anymore.[82]

This is not the same as repressing your anger. That is harmful: to push it down into the subconscious without resolving it by making it a sacrifice for sin. If you repress it, it may explode someday. Not good.

I know a person who has moved on so well from the things that made him angry that he can hardly remember what those things were. He has a lot of peace. Dwelling on unpleasant feelings can ruin our peace and joy.

This is not to say that anger is the *only* feeling we may have to deal with. It could be that we have feelings of guilt, or of remorse, or any number of other feelings. Let's deal with these one at a time.

*Guilt*: a feeling of shame or self-reproach. Feeling guilty after we have sinned is a *good* thing, as we mentioned in an earlier chapter. It should move us to repent, confess our sin, and make amends. If the feeling remains, again, just give it to God as reparation for sin in the world — over and over again if necessary. If we choose to keep the feeling of guilt, it could be the result of pride.

*Resentment*: a feeling of offense or indignation over a perceived wrong. This is what some people feel toward their spouses sometimes. It's not a Christian virtue. But it is a valid feeling at times. This is another destroyer of peace. There are two spiritual works of mercy that can be used to process this feeling: bearing injustices patiently and forgiving all injuries. As with many things that bring us great grace, this goes against our natural tendencies. And it can be a destroyer of pride, which is the root of all sin. If we

---

[82] For more details on handling anger, see my book *Overcoming Sinful Anger* (Manchester, NH: Sophia Institute Press, 2015).

are going to live this, we must take a deep breath and remember why we are doing it: to make reparation for sins, to imitate Jesus (how many injustices He endured!), and to live in peace with all men and women. Hanging on to resentment will prevent us from finding peace in our lives and will sour our relationships.

*Sadness over the Church*: a number of people have succumbed to sadness, anger, or disgust over the shameful misbehavior of some of our priests and bishops. There was an analogous crisis among priests and bishops in the thirteenth century. Although the sins of the late twentieth and early twenty-first centuries were worse than those of the thirteenth century, the latter sins were very serious and were committed publicly, with no shame. A good number of priests were living openly with their mistresses or their "wives." Many priests were involved in seeking money for themselves and having a good time. They hardly preached at all, virtually never studied, and paid for important positions so that they could get even more money. Some of the bishops lived in unbelievable wealth and would sell Church positions to keep their luxurious lifestyle. The Church was suffering greatly from the shameful behavior of her leaders.

Along came many reformers, including Peter Waldo. He gave up his riches to live in poverty and spread the Faith. He had many followers who also lived as poor men and did penance. However, when they began to preach without permission against the lazy and sinful priests, the archbishop of Lyons, France, excommunicated them.

The group, called the Waldensians, took their case to the pope, who encouraged them. At first, he gave Peter and his followers permission to urge reform wherever the bishops allowed them to do so. But since they had not studied theology, they were not permitted to explain the Bible or to instruct people in the Faith. Unfortunately, they did both and, eventually, without the bishops' permission.

In time, they got into all sorts of errors, claiming their interpretation of the Bible to be better than the pope's, and denying both purgatory and the veneration of the saints. As a result, the Waldensians were excommunicated by the pope in 1184.

In all fairness, these reformers were holier than many of the bishops they criticized. But they made one crucial error: they disobeyed the bishops and the pope. Disobedience is never a part of holiness.

In the early thirteenth century, another reformer appeared who also lived great poverty and humility. He and his followers preached the gospel all over but never spoke against priests or bishops by name.[83] Rather, they honored even the laziest and most immoral of them, because they represented Christ Himself (despite their sinfulness). If a bishop told them they could not teach in his diocese, they left. The name of this reformer was Francis of Assisi. He and his followers were completely obedient. These humble men and women (including the Poor Clares) totally reformed the Church in just eighteen years.

These stories illustrate a surprising fact about Christ's Catholic Church. Even when many of her leaders are corrupt, Christ is far more with His Church than He is with otherwise holy reformers who refuse to obey the Church. The corrupt leaders who do not repent and reform will reap misery for themselves, but Christ remains with His Church.

The point is that the Church has known shameful corruption on the part of some of her leaders in the past, but God has raised

---

[83] St. Anthony, one of Francis's followers, ruthlessly criticized priests and bishops but never mentioned their names.

up saints to bring about reform. It will not be different in this age. Our task is to become saints and to be part of the reform. No corrupt Church leader can keep us from becoming holy. We have so many examples to follow in the history of the Church, saints about whom we can read. Lamenting the bad examples of our leaders for any extended period is, in the end, a waste of time. We each have the mission to contribute to the reform of the Church by first pursuing holiness in our own lives and then working to promote genuine reform.

*Envy*: a desire to possess the goods of another to the extent that you would wish the other harm. If you read the life of St. Francis of Assisi, you should never feel envious of anyone again. His whole approach to life was to be the poorest, lowliest person on earth. And because of that, he was one of the happiest! He became so Christlike that he miraculously received the *stigmata*, the wounds of Christ in his hands and feet. He is a good saint to try to imitate, even if only in a limited way.[84]

*Anxiety*: a feeling of uneasiness or distress. The antidote to this feeling is *trust*. There are scores of Scripture passages extolling the virtue of trust. For example:

> He who dwells in the shelter of the Most High ... will say to the Lord, "My refuge and my fortress; my God, in whom I trust." ... A thousand may fall at your side, ten thousand at your right hand; but it will not come near you.... For he will give his angels charge of you to guard you in all

---

[84] For a short account of St. Francis's life, see my book *Who's Who in Heaven: Real Saints for Families in Plain English* (Steubenville: Emmaus Road, 2012). For a longer account of the life of St. Francis, I recommend Omer Englebert, *St. Francis of Assisi: A Biography* (Ann Arbor: Servant Books, 1979).

your ways. On their hands they shall bear you up, lest you dash your foot against a stone. (Ps. 91:1–12, RSVCE)

Jesus told St. Maria Faustina, "The graces of My mercy are drawn by means of one vessel only, and that is trust. The more a soul trusts, the more it will receive. Souls that trust boundlessly are a great comfort to Me, because I pour all the treasures of My grace into them."[85] He also told her, "Sins of distrust wound me most painfully."[86] It is not just in exercising our will that we come to trust in God and all that He allows to happen in our lives. It calls for us to pray as well: "Lord, teach me to trust." I read several excerpts on trust from Scripture daily and then ask the Lord to teach me this virtue — every day!

One young man asked me, "Father, Sts. Peter and Paul trusted in God, and yet they were still martyred. What good was their trust?" I answered, "Trusting in God does not guarantee that something bad won't happen to you. The martyrdom of Peter and Paul was part of God's will for them. Great good came out of their deaths, for the faith of the people, and for their own sanctity. Trusting in God will not keep us from every bad thing. But if we trust in God, whatever happens will be for the good, our good and the good of the world." Remember, the greatest goods are spiritual, not physical or worldly.

*Grief*: deep sorrow. There are several books available on the importance of grieving the loss of a loved one.[87] We should grieve

---

[85] Sister Sophia Michalenko, *Mercy My Mission: Life of Sister Faustina H. Kowalska* (Stockbridge, MA: Marian Press, 1987), 215.

[86] *Diary*, no. 1076.

[87] One that has stood the test of time is *A Grief Observed* by C. S. Lewis, first published in 1961 and still number two on the Christian Death and Grief list on Amazon.

over such a loss, but not forever. There comes a time when we have to move on and live the rest of our lives. When she was twenty-eight years old, St. Jane Frances de Chantal lost her husband in a hunting accident. She was crushed to see her eight-year idyllic marriage come to an end. She spent the next four months grieving, until a letter from her father revived her by reminding her of her duties to her children. She realized at that point that the happiness of this world was of little importance, and it passes quickly. She gave her life over to pleasing the Lord and helping His people.

*Bitterness*: a feeling characterized by sharpness, anger, and resentment. For example, this feeling may arise in the case of a person whose spouse runs off with a lover (and too often moves in with him or her). In this situation, bitterness is almost inevitable. The question is, will this bitterness take over? There should come a time when the one betrayed says, "Enough. He (or she) ruined my marriage, but he (or she) will not ruin my life."

*Fear*: a feeling of alarm in anticipation of danger. "What if this happens ... or that? Then I would be ruined. And what if this happens?" We have all fallen into this irrational way of thinking. The devil loves this. He is more than willing to suggest all sorts of things that *could* happen but probably won't. Christians have a way to deal with this: trust. Again, it is not easy to get into the habit of trust. We need to pray for it.

*Moods*: uneven emotional states. We all have moods from time to time. Women have more reasons to have moods because their chemistry changes so dramatically each month. Those who give in to their moods and let them dominate their hearts often make those around them miserable. When we see we are having a mood, we should catch ourselves and say, "I need to compensate for this and try extra hard to be pleasant and kind." The love we Christians should have for all those around us calls for this.

*Fatigue*: a feeling of exhaustion and weariness. When we are tired, we can become cranky. As with moods, we should work to compensate for being tired when we become aware of it and make every effort to be pleasant.

*Selfish feelings*: a feeling of placing oneself over others. I know very few selfish Christians. To be selfish is to want to satisfy one's own desires no matter what it costs others. That's *desires*, not needs. A small example of that would be when a person takes the last five cookies, knowing that others haven't had any and would certainly like some. Of course, when we were young, we might have often done that, but with good parents we learned that that is not an acceptable way to behave. That is Unselfishness 101.

What I have seen more often is Christians who feel selfish about taking care of their true needs while not inconveniencing others. For example, one mother told me she feared she was being selfish playing tennis twice a week, in light of the fact that she has five children. I asked if her children were deprived by it. She said no. I said, "Then it's good that you play tennis twice a week. It will help you sleep better, your overall health—physical and psychological—will be better, and you will have some natural friendships. Your playing tennis might be a blessing for your children since you will be better able to serve them."

Kathryn Sansone, a lovely young mother of ten, urges mothers to care for themselves so they can serve their families better. She writes that, after a few years of marriage, "I began to understand that unless I took care of myself, everything in life would seem too difficult, too unmanageable, and definitely not enjoyable.... Was I ready to take care of myself, or would I let myself get pulled down the road where a negative, powerless attitude toward life holds sway? I chose the former and it has made all the difference."[88]

Here's what Kathryn suggests: Take a nice warm bath to relax before bed. She lights some candles for the occasion. She suggests taking a walk in a nature reserve; or driving out into the country; or taking a nap; or getting a massage; or going to the gym. Sometimes she "hibernates"—that is, she cancels all but the bare-bones necessities, she skips the gym and just rests for one, two, or more days. An essential part of her program is to learn to say no to people. And she gets help from others when she needs it. As a devout Catholic, she makes time for prayer, either alone (in various settings) or with her family. This woman has ten children, and she is not burning herself out!

Is it selfish for women to take time for themselves? No. It's a virtue to get the sleep, the recreation, and other care you need. It is part of the virtue of humility: "I know I have some needs and that I am not superwoman."

*Negativity*: a point of view that stresses the bad aspects of a situation, a person, or another entity. We can all get into this attitude at times. One way to overcome it is to write the word *negativity* on an index card as something to overcome. Then look at the card each morning and night to remind yourself that you want to overcome that feeling and the behavior it leads to. At night, say an Act of Contrition just after reading the card. Seeing it written will help you to keep aware of the need to dismiss those feelings before they drag you—and everyone around you—into the pits.

---

[88] Kathryn Sansone, *Woman First, Family Always* (Des Moines, IA: Meredith Books, 2006), 19.

# Overcoming Sinful Thoughts

∞

The point of all this is, you need not be pulled down by negative feelings. Just acknowledge the bad feeling, do what you can to alleviate it, and then move on. Enjoy your blessings.

15

# "There Can Be No God in a World with So Much Suffering"

The husband of one of my parishioners witnessed some of the horror left behind in France after World War II. He was so deeply hurt by what he saw that he couldn't relate to a God who would allow such suffering and destruction. He ceased going to Mass and praying. He died some years later, without being reconciled to the Lord.

While his sensitivity was commendable, his response was not. His behavior highlights the difficult question: Why is there so much suffering? Why does God permit it?

## Types of Suffering

Suffering is something that touches each of our lives. Although much suffering is ultimately mysterious to our limited human minds, there are several causes or reasons behind suffering that we can perceive. Distinguishing the different types of suffering can help us to begin to understand this difficult aspect of human existence.

# Overcoming Sinful Thoughts

## *Suffering Caused by Us*

The kind of suffering with the most obvious cause is the suffering we bring on ourselves. Because God wants us to love freely, He allows us the freedom to choose good or evil, love or selfishness. These choices have consequences.

When a person has chosen to get high on recreational drugs and become addicted, he must take the consequences. He may lose his job, his health, his spouse, and even his family members. He suffers because the world has a moral order, whereby choosing the good will ultimately produce good, and choosing evil will bring about evil or suffering. He chose the evil of recreational drugs under the appearance of the good feeling he would get, and he got that good feeling. However, that came at a price — a high price because he failed to account for the downside of taking drugs. And, for most people in our contemporary world, it is a downside that is easily knowable. The dangers of taking drugs are well documented by the media. To be unaware of them is almost impossible in our world of ubiquitous communication.

If a person robs a bank, he will very likely get caught and will have to suffer imprisonment. No surprise.

So, that's the easiest type of suffering to understand. If we make bad choices, we suffer.

## *The Suffering of Victims*

When Adolf Hitler carried out his evil program, he caused a large number of innocent victims to suffer. "Not fair!" we protest. Regarding fairness, we should reconcile ourselves to the fact that we often don't receive fairness in this world. For the Christian, this is not totally catastrophic, since there is a life to come and there we will find justice.

There are many reasons people suffer, even when they don't "deserve" it according to our standards of fairness. For starters, suffering in the world is related to sin. St. John Paul II put it this way:

> And even if we must use great caution in judging man's suffering as a consequence of concrete sins (this is shown precisely by the example of the just man Job), nevertheless suffering cannot be divorced from the sin of the beginnings, from what Saint John calls "the sin of the world" [John 1:29], from the sinful background of the personal actions and social processes in human history. Though it is not licit to apply here the narrow criterion of direct dependence (as Job's three friends did), it is equally true that one cannot reject the criterion that, at the basis of human suffering, there is a complex involvement with sin.[89]

In other words, because there is sin in the world, there is suffering in the world. This is dramatically shown in the suffering of Jesus on the Cross. He suffered not because of *His* sin but because of *our* sins.

Some would suggest that His suffering was enough. We should not have to suffer as well. However, this is not borne out in Sacred Scripture. St. Paul wrote, "Now I rejoice in my sufferings for your sake, and in my flesh I am completing what is lacking in Christ's afflictions for the sake of his body, that is, the church" (Col. 1:24, RSVCE).

How could anything be lacking in the sufferings of Christ? There couldn't be anything lacking, insofar as Christ's sufferings

---

[89] Pope John Paul II, Apostolic Letter *Salvifici Doloris* (On the Christian Meaning of Human Suffering) (February 11, 1984), no. 15.

achieved what was intended. But it seems that what was intended was for Christ to atone for the infinite dimension of sin, something we could not hope to do as finite beings. The infinite dimension of sin would be the infinite injustice of a creature sinning against a completely good and loving God.

However, for the finite dimension of sin, the harm our sin has done to others and to ourselves, it appears that we are called to atone for at least a part of that evil. St. Paul's words seem to point clearly to the necessity of this reparation on our part. The experience of the saints is a testament to the truth that suffering affects us all. St. Thérèse of Lisieux, in her final agony before she died, called out, "I could never have believed it was possible to suffer so much.... There are no consolations, not even one! It is because of my desire to save souls."[90] When the saints suffered, they doubled down on their commitment to Christ and suffered heroically. The final weeks of St. Maximilian Kolbe in the concentration camp were a wonderful example of that.

Jesus' death is the quintessential explanation of suffering. There is suffering because there is sin. As St. John Paul II said, our suffering may not be due to our own sin, but it is somehow related to the sin of the world.

The *Catechism of the Catholic Church* teaches, "The cross is the unique sacrifice of Christ, the 'one mediator between God and men.' But because in his incarnate divine person he has in some way united himself to every man, 'the possibility of being made partners, in a way known to God, in the paschal mystery' is offered to all men. He calls his disciples to 'take up [their] cross and follow (him)' (Matt. 16:24)" (618).

---

[90] Christopher O'Mahony, *St. Thérèse of Lisieux by Those Who Knew Her* (Dublin: Veritas, 1975), 105.

St. John Paul II wrote, "In bringing about the Redemption through suffering, Christ raised human suffering to the level of the Redemption. Thus each man, in his sufferings, can also become a sharer in the redemptive suffering of Christ."[91] For those who embrace their sufferings, those sufferings are redemptive; they share in the redemptive mission of Christ when they unite their suffering to that of Christ on the Cross.

We might speculate about how redemptive suffering can make up for sin. Sin is an affirmation of self in a denial of love. Redemptive suffering is an affirmation of love in a denial of self.

There are two kinds of redemptive suffering: active and passive. Active suffering is that which we choose: for example, fasting, or kneeling for a long period of time. Passive suffering is present when we embrace our sicknesses, injuries, or heartbreaks. St. Francis de Sales gave a higher value to the latter because there is more of God's will therein.

## Vicarious Suffering

One of the most difficult questions often posed is why infants suffer. It seems they could hardly be guilty of personal sin. This is a special case of suffering by those who seem not to have sinned; that is, vicarious suffering.

The saints agreed to suffer vicariously. Others, including infants, suffer without being asked. What can we say of that? Certainly there is mystery here, but we might speculate that the doctrine of God's knowledge of *futuribilia*, might come into play in this situation. Futuribilia is the knowledge of what will not actually occur but would happen if certain conditions were fulfilled. It is based on the words of Jesus: "Woe to you, Chorazin!

[91] Pope John Paul II, *Salvifici Doloris*, no. 19.

Woe to you, Bethsaida! For if the deeds of power done in you had been done in Tyre and Sidon, they would have repented long ago in sackcloth and ashes" (Matt. 11:21).

So God could know how a person would respond if he were asked to suffer vicariously for the sins of others. This, of course, is just a clue, not an answer. Mystery must prevail here.

Another point worth making: we are quite ready to accept the vicarious sufferings of Christ for our sins (since we ourselves could never make a dent in the infinite debt of sin). Is it unfair for God to have us share in the mission of Christ? As we saw earlier, St. Paul said he shared in that mission (Col. 1:24). I mean, if we suffer vicariously without being asked, does God then owe us for our suffering, in light of what His own Son suffered vicariously for us?

There is another clue regarding infants: the feast of the Holy Innocents. They are considered saints in the Church. Could other infants who suffered be seen by God as saints?

To be sure, all of this is quite tentative. The last thing I want to do is pretend to solve the mystery that Job was told was unsolvable. The definitive solution to that mystery will have to wait until we meet the Lord. But these might qualify as helpful hints.

### Natural Disasters

A final form of suffering in the victimhood category is that caused by natural disasters: earthquakes, tsunamis, hurricanes, and so forth. All that suffering—how could a good God allow it? Couldn't He prevent these things?

It seems that He could. God caused the plagues in Egypt to force Pharaoh to let the Israelites go free. God caused the flood in the time of Noah. God withheld the destruction of Nineveh when its inhabitants repented. Nowhere in Sacred

Scripture does God appear to be helpless in the face of natural disasters. To the contrary, it repeatedly affirms His power: "Does disaster befall a city, unless the Lord has done it?" (Amos 3:6); "Then the Lord said to [Moses], 'Who gives speech to mortals? Who makes them mute or deaf, seeing or blind? Is it not I, the Lord?'" (Exod. 4:11); "There is no god besides me. I kill and I make alive; I wound and I heal; and no one can deliver from my hand" (Deut. 32:39).[92]

It is here that Rabbi Kushner, writing in his popular *When Bad Things Happen to Good People*, falls short. He claims that God cannot control everything. God *does* have the power to prevent natural disasters, as is indicated in Job, but His reasons are beyond Job's comprehension. Peter Kreeft, in his excellent work *Making Sense Out of Suffering*, takes Kushner to task for his incorrect interpretation of Job: "Job's lesson is that suffering is a mystery, but Kushner insists on rationality. Job teaches humility, Kushner insists on an answer. God himself tells Job he can't know, but Kushner insists on knowing. Job's God asserts his omnipotence; Kushner not only denies his omnipotence but asserts that the Book of Job denies it too."[93]

The book of Job is a key text in revealing the nature of suffering. Job loses his children, his fortune, and his property through marauders and natural disasters. He complains or at least wonders how he can suffer so much despite the fact that he is a pretty decent person. He deems his suffering excessive and undeserved.

---

[92] See John Piper, "The Sovereignty of God," Desiring God, November 3, 2012, https://www.desiringgod.org/messages/the-sovereignty-of-god-my-counsel-shall-stand-and-i-will-accomplish-all-my-purpose.

[93] Peter Kreeft, *Making Sense Out of Suffering* (Cincinnati: Servant Books, 1986), 48.

After Job's three friends try unsuccessfully to convince him to admit his sins and accept his punishment, Elihu takes another approach. He tells Job not to think that suffering comes only from one's sins. He proclaims:

> For God speaks in one way,
>> and in two, though people do not perceive it.
> In a dream, in a vision of the night,
>> when deep sleep falls on mortals,
>> while they slumber on their beds,
> then he opens their ears,
>> and terrifies them with warnings,
> that he may turn them aside from their deeds,
>> and keep them from pride,
> to spare their souls from the Pit,
>> their lives from traversing the River.
> (Job 33:14–18)

So God warns people, tries to turn them from their bad behavior, to turn them from pride and keep them from losing their souls by dying in their sins. Suffering can have the salutary effect of reorienting us to God.

Kreeft points to the argument of Boethius, an influential philosopher of the sixth century. Boethius argues that ill fortune is better for us than good fortune. He points out that good fortune poses as happiness, but it isn't. "When the worldly toys in which we place our hopes are taken away from us, our foolishness is also taken away, and this brings us closer to true happiness, which is not in worldly things but in wisdom.... We need truth more than comfort."[94]

---

[94] Kreeft, *Making Sense Out of Suffering*, 70.

The assumption of the worldly person is that suffering is the worst thing in the world. But from a religious perspective, it isn't. Kreeft refers to C.S. Lewis to point out that the soul is more important than the body. Bodily goods include health, pleasure, and the avoidance of suffering. What are goods of the soul? Wisdom, humility, compassion, holiness, and other virtues. If we must suffer to attain virtues, and it seems we must, then suffering is not all bad. It is a lesser evil that produces a greater good.[95]

## Clues to God's Reasons

Recognizing that, ultimately, God's reasons are a mystery, there are nonetheless some clues that offer insight into those reasons. I have already hinted at some of them; here are some more.

### The Blind Man

There is a curious passage in Sacred Scripture about the healing of a blind man: "As he walked along, [Jesus] saw a man blind from birth. His disciples asked him, 'Rabbi, who sinned, this man or his parents, that he was born blind?' Jesus answered, 'Neither this man nor his parents sinned; he was born blind so that God's works might be revealed in him'" (John 9:1–3). And then Jesus healed him.

One might ask how the sin of a man born blind could have caused his blindness. In fact, there was a belief among some at the time that a person could sin in the womb, before birth.[96]

---

[95] Kreeft, *Making Sense Out of* Suffering, 71–72.
[96] *William Barclay's Daily Study Bible*, John 9, StudyLight.org, https://www.studylight.org/commentaries/dsb/john-9.html.

More importantly, in response to their question as to whether his blindness was due to his own sin or that of his parents, Jesus replies that it was neither. His being born blind was "so that God's works might be revealed in him." In other words, the man was born blind so that Jesus could heal him, thereby allowing him and others to witness God's healing power. How many souls were saved as a result of Jesus' miracle? It might seem to us that this was a great hardship for the man to endure to make possible this "sign" from our Lord. However, compared with the saving of one soul, not to mention several souls, for all eternity, this man's great hardship seems less harsh.

### Lost in the Temple

Another curious instance of suffering is that endured by our Blessed Mother and St. Joseph when Jesus was lost in the Temple. How difficult it must have been for them to search for Him for those three days. It is suggested that they could neither eat nor sleep during this trial. When they finally found him, Mary asked,

> "Child, why have you treated us like this? Look, your father and I have been searching for you in great anxiety." He said to them, "Why were you searching for me? Did you not know that I must be about my Father's interests?" But they did not understand what he said to them. Then he went down with them and came to Nazareth, and was obedient to them. His mother treasured all these things in her heart. (Luke 2:48–51)

We might wonder why Mary and Joseph had to endure this trial. Perhaps the most plausible answer is that given by the visionary Maria of Agreda. She suggested that the scholars were discussing the Messiah and whether he had already entered the world. They based their speculation on the extraordinary events surrounding the birth of John the Baptist and the advent of the three kings some twelve years before. They wondered, would the Messiah come as an earthly king or a suffering servant? According to Maria, Jesus had gently offered: "Could it not be that the Messiah will come twice, once to redeem the world, and again to judge it?"

If that is true, Jesus' obligation to plant that seed in the minds of the Jewish teachers took precedence over the peace of His parents. And, of course, the suffering of these two holy persons would be united to the redemptive sufferings Jesus Himself would endure for the salvation of mankind.

### The Trials of the Chosen People

Another aspect of suffering is found in the book of Judith:

> In spite of everything let us give thanks to the Lord our God, who is putting us to the test as he did our ancestors. Remember what he did with Abraham, and how he tested Isaac, and what happened to Jacob in Syrian Mesopotamia, while he was tending the sheep of Laban, his mother's brother. For he has not tried us with fire, as he did them, to search their hearts, nor has he taken vengeance on us; but the Lord scourges those who are close to him in order to admonish them. (Jth. 8:25-27 RSVCE)

Here we see examples of God putting His people to the test at various times in history and in various ways to "admonish" them. This coincides with the theme of God's disciplining His children:

> Endure hardship as discipline; God is treating you as his children. For what children are not disciplined by

their father? If you are not disciplined—and everyone undergoes discipline—then you are not legitimate, not true sons and daughters at all. Moreover, we have all had human fathers who disciplined us and we respected them for it. How much more should we submit to the Father of spirits and live? (Heb. 12:7–9, NIV)[97]

God punishes, as a good father does, to correct his child.

## Responding to Suffering

Whether we can fully understand God's reasons or not, suffering comes to all of us. We must respond to it in some fashion. There are at least two typical responses to suffering. The first is to rail against it and the God who permits it. The second is to do what the saints did: to embrace it as a cross and unite it to the sufferings of Christ on the Cross. The latter is the redemptive suffering described above. It is that suffering that St. Paul rejoiced in to make up what was lacking in the sufferings of Christ. Those who take this path can make reparation for the sins of mankind and even save souls from perdition.[98] St. John Paul II proclaimed, "The Cross is the cradle of the new man."[99]

This is, no doubt, why the writers of Sacred Scripture invite us to find consolation in our sufferings: "Rejoice insofar as you share Christ's sufferings, so that you may also be glad and shout for joy when his glory is revealed" (1 Pet. 4:13, RSVCE). "For

[97] See also Proverbs 3:12ff., and Revelation 3:19ff., among others.
[98] William Thomas Walsh, *Our Lady of Fatima* (New York: Doubleday, 1990), 120.
[99] *The Whole Truth about Man: John Paul II to University Faculties and Students* (Boston: St. Paul Editions, 1981), 121.

just as the sufferings of Christ are abundant for us, so also our consolation is abundant through Christ" (2 Cor. 1:5). "And not only that, but we also boast in our sufferings, knowing that suffering produces endurance, and endurance produces character, and character produces hope, and hope does not disappoint us, because God's love has been poured into our hearts through the Holy Spirit that has been given to us" (Rom. 5:3–5).

Even those who rail against their suffering can gain something spiritual. They can grow in humility, as Elihu proclaimed in the book of Job, and as St. Augustine suggested in *The City of God*.[100] The person who suffers learns, even if subconsciously, that he cannot control everything. Against certain things or in certain situations, he is powerless. That realization is the entrée to humility.

As Augustine also taught, humility is a virtue that is indispensable to living a moral life: "If you ask me what is the most essential element in the teaching and morality of Jesus Christ, I would answer you: the first is humility, the second is humility, and the third is humility."[101] In the light of eternity, for those with a supernatural outlook, suffering is a small price to pay for the key but elusive virtue of humility.

There is another benefit in suffering for those who rail against God over their misery: it makes clear just what their fundamental orientation is—for or against God. People can go along attending weekly Mass and praying a bit but at heart be only lukewarmly

---

[100] St. Augustine, *City of God*, bk. 1, chap. 28. Here Augustine suggests that the women who were violated by the barbarians could have advanced in humility by this travesty.

[101] Letter 118, 22; quoted in "Humility, Source of Joy," August 26, 2008, Opus Dei, http://www.opusdei.us/art.php?p=29262.

committed to the Lord. When they suffer, their response makes it clear, especially to them, where their treasure lies.

Hopefully, by putting suffering within this supernatural outlook, we should be able to say to ourselves, "If I am not on the path to holiness and salvation, I would very much value a wake-up call, making clear just how far I am off the right path, however painful." Painful, but valuable. In *The Problem of Pain*, C. S. Lewis wrote, "God whispers in our pleasures but shouts in our pain. Pain is his megaphone to rouse a dulled world."

## The Value of Suffering

"I plan to be the first person to become a saint without suffering."

Yes, someone actually said this to me—someone who has read many lives of the saints, not to mention the Gospels. I believe it was totally tongue-in-cheek, but it was still an amazing statement.

I won't dignify this with a detailed rebuttal, but here are some pertinent quotes. "[Jesus] summoned the crowd with his disciples and said to them, 'Whoever wishes to come after me must deny himself, take up his cross, and follow me. For whoever wishes to save his life will lose it, but whoever loses his life for my sake and that of the gospel will save it'" (Mark 8:34–35). St. Augustine wrote, "Our pilgrimage on earth cannot be exempt from trial. We progress by means of trial. No one knows himself except through trial or receives a crown except after victory, or strives except against an enemy or temptations."[102]

---

[102] Easter Office of Readings, First Sunday of Lent, *Liturgy of the Hours*, vol. 2.

## The Wounds of Christ

There is a key teaching in the stigmata, the wounds of Christ bestowed on several saints, including St. Francis of Assisi and St. Padre Pio: to share in the sufferings of Christ is an honor. St. Paul wrote, "May I never glory except in the cross of our Lord Jesus Christ, through which the world has been crucified to me and I to the world" (Gal. 6:14).

Many spiritual writers have stressed the importance of suffering as part of the Christian life. Archbishop Fulton Sheen proclaimed: "When the devil is stripped of all his trappings, the ultimate goal of the demonic is to avoid the Cross, mortification, self-discipline and self-denial."[103] Jesus told Rose of Lima that, "without the cross [souls] can find no road to climb to heaven."[104] Teresa of Ávila wrote, "God treats His friends terribly; yet in truth he does them no wrong, for he dealt likewise with his son."[105]

Some of the saints even sought out suffering as a path to holiness. St. André Bessette said, "If we only knew the value of suffering we would fall on our knees and ask it of God."[106] St. John of the Cross asked for three things: first, that he might suffer something each day; second, that he might not die as a superior

---

[103] Fulton J. Sheen, *Treasure in Clay: The Autobiography of Fulton J. Sheen* (New York: Doubleday, 1980), 334.

[104] Quoted in "Unfathomable Treasure of Grace—Rose of Lima," Crossroads Initiative, https://www.crossroadsinitiative.com/media/articles/rose-lima-grace-august-23/.

[105] "Letter to Padre Jerónimo Gracián," as quoted in William Thomas Walsh, *St. Teresa of Ávila, Reformer of Carmel* (Rockford, IL: TAN Books, 1999).

[106] From a special issue on Saint Brother André *The Guardian of Crusaders*, Bulletin of the Eucharistic Crusade for Canada, no. 207 (October 2010): 10, http://fsspx.com/EucharisticCrusade/2010_October_print.pdf.

in his Carmelite Order; and third, that he might end his life in humiliation, disgrace, and contempt. It seems he was granted all three. He told his brother once that, one night as he prayed before a picture of Jesus on His way to Calvary, the Lord said to him, "John, ask what favor you will have of me, and I will grant it in return for the services you have done me." John's answer was, "Lord, make me suffer for your sake, and be despised and regarded as worthless." He wrote, "Suffering for God is better than working miracles."[107]

Should we ask for suffering as did St. John? Yes, it is part of our liturgical prayer. For example, in the intercessions for Morning Prayer in the Divine Office, Easter Sunday, we can read: "Lord, you walked the way of suffering and crucifixion; may we suffer and die with you and rise again to share your glory." And, in the opening prayer for the Mass of St. Philip the Apostle (May 3) we find, "God our Father, every year you give us joy on the festival of the Apostles Philip and James. By the help of their prayers may we share in the suffering, death and resurrection of your Son and come to the eternal vision of your glory."[108] *Lex orandi, lex credenda* — the norm of prayer is the norm of belief.

This positive response makes sense especially when we consider that suffering comes to all, regardless of sanctity. Paradoxically, embracing suffering as a Christian is less painful than resisting it as meaningless. As St. John Vianney taught, suffering

---

[107] St. John of the Cross, *Other Counsels*, no. 13.

[108] There are other examples, such as the closing prayer for the Mass of the Holy Rosary (October 7); Evening Prayer, Friday, week 3, closing prayer; and Morning Prayer, Second Wednesday of Lent, final intercession.

for Christ is easier than seeking happiness in the world: "You have less to suffer in following the cross than in serving the world and its pleasures."[109]

## Should We Pray for Healing?

If suffering is so valuable, is it acceptable to pray to avoid it? Should we pray, for example, for healing from a sickness or an ailment? Yes, absolutely. We read in the Letter of James:

> Are any among you sick? They should call for the elders of the church and have them pray over them, anointing them with oil in the name of the Lord. The prayer of faith will save the sick, and the Lord will raise them up; and anyone who has committed sins will be forgiven. Therefore confess your sins to one another, and pray for one another, so that you may be healed. The prayer of the righteous is powerful and effective. (James 5:14–16)

The sacrament of Anointing of the Sick is based on this passage. A good number of people have experienced healing upon receiving this sacrament.

And in 1 Corinthians we find: "To each is given the manifestation of the Spirit for the common good. To one is given through the Spirit the utterance of wisdom, and to another the utterance of knowledge according to the same Spirit, to another faith by the same Spirit, to another gifts of healing by the one Spirit" (1 Cor. 12:7–9).

---

[109] Quoted in Francis W. Johnston, *The Voice of the Saints: Counsels from the Saints to Bring Comfort and Guidance in Daily Living* (Rockford, IL: TAN Books, 1986), chap. 2.

Our blessed Lord performed many healings, as did the apostles after Jesus' death and resurrection. For example, Peter healed a lame beggar:

> Peter said [to the beggar] "I have no silver or gold, but what I have I give you; in the name of Jesus Christ of Nazareth, stand up and walk." And he took him by the right hand and raised him up; and immediately his feet and ankles were made strong. Jumping up, he stood and began to walk, and he entered the temple with them, walking and leaping and praising God. (Acts 3:6–8)

And, later in Acts, we read "that they even carried out the sick into the streets, and laid them on cots and mats, in order that Peter's shadow might fall on some of them as he came by. A great number of people would also gather from the towns around Jerusalem, bringing the sick and those tormented by unclean spirits, and they were all cured" (Acts 5:15–16).

It seems Jesus used His healings, and those of His saints, to help people realize that He was divine and that they should embrace His gospel.

St. John Bosco, spiritual father to thousands of young boys, became very sick with pneumonia in 1846. His friend Fr. Borel gave John Viaticum[110] and then Anointing of the Sick. It looked as if he would die. The boys prayed and fasted for John's healing. At one point, Fr. Borel urged John to pray for his own recovery. John was not sure he should, saying, "Let God's will be done." "Yes, but think of the boys. What would they do if they lost you?" asked his friend. John was convinced by that argument and prayed

---

[110] Viaticum is the final reception of Holy Communion before death.

on the spot for his own recovery, "Lord, if it pleases You, let me be healed." His prayers were effective. The following day, his doctor pronounced the young priest on his way to recovery. He would need three more months of rest, staying with his mother in Becchi, but he recovered completely.[111]

So yes, we should pray for healing. Although our suffering is of great value, at times God answers our prayers for healing as a sign of His presence. How many people have had their faith boosted, and in some cases restored, by the healing of a person as a result of prayers! And if we should receive a healing, we should be willing to tell of it to all who will listen.

Granted, many prayers for healing do not receive a positive answer. But when they do, we should shout it from the rooftops.

## Trust

A dear friend sometimes asks me, "Why does God permit this terrible thing?" Of course, there is never an easy answer, but the Sacred Scriptures proclaim:

> For my thoughts are not your thoughts,
> nor are your ways my ways, says the LORD.
> For as the heavens are higher than the earth,
> so are my ways higher than your ways
> and my thoughts than your thoughts. (Isa. 55:8–9)

When we are perplexed at things that have happened, we must turn to the virtue God ardently wants us to have: trust.

One of the most consoling verses in Sacred Scripture is found in Romans: "All things work out for good for those who love

---

[111] Morrow, *Who's Who in Heaven*, 48–49.

God" (Rom. 8:28). This is illustrated by the following dialogue, which has been handed down for years.

MAN. God, can I ask You a question?

GOD. Sure.

MAN. Promise You won't get mad.

GOD. I promise.

MAN. Why did You let so much stuff happen to me today?

GOD. What do you mean?

MAN. Well, I woke up late.

GOD. Yes.

MAN. My car took forever to start.

GOD. Okay.

MAN. At lunch they made my sandwich wrong, and I had to wait.

GOD. Hmm.

MAN. On the way home, my phone went dead, just as I picked up a call!

GOD. All right.

MAN. And on top of it all, when I got home, I just wanted to soak my feet in my new foot massager and relax—but it wouldn't work! Nothing went right today. Why did You do that?

GOD. Let me see. The death angel was at your bed this morning, and I had to send one of my angels to battle him for your life. I let you sleep through that.

MAN (humbled). Oh.

GOD. I didn't let your car start because there was a drunk driver on your route who would have hit you if you were on the road.

(Man is silent, ashamed.)

GOD. The first person who made your sandwich today was sick, and I didn't want you to catch what he had. I knew you couldn't afford to miss work.

MAN (*embarrassed*). Okay.

GOD. Your phone went dead because the person calling was going to give false witness about what you said on that call. I didn't even let you talk to him so you would be covered.

MAN (*softly*). I see, God.

GOD. Oh, and that foot massager, it had a short in it, and that was going to throw out all of the power in your house tonight. I didn't think you wanted to be in the dark.

MAN. I'm sorry, God.

GOD. Don't be sorry; just learn to trust me — in all things, the good and the bad.

MAN. I will trust You.

GOD. And don't doubt that my plan for your day is always better than your plan.

MAN. I won't, God. And let me just tell You, God: thank You for everything today.

GOD. You're welcome, child. It was just another day being your God and looking after my children.

The following story is another short illustration of why we should trust.

There was a man marooned on an island. Because on cool nights the wind made it difficult for him to sleep, he went around the island gathering wood to build himself a little hut. He put a hole in the roof so he could have a fire in his hut.

One day, he went to gather some food on the other side of the island. Unfortunately, he left a few embers in his fire before he left. Upon returning, he was horrified to see that his hut was burning to the ground. He looked up to Heaven and shook his fist, asking, "God, how could You let this happen? I have been praying to You every day asking for Your help, and this is what I get?" As he continued to complain, he noticed a small motorboat appear and come to shore. It had come from a ship about a mile out. The men in the boat shouted to him, "We saw your fire. What a smart idea! Without that fire, we would never have found you!" He was rescued.

Cardinal John Henry Newman wrote of his trust as follows:

> If I am in sickness my sickness may serve him;
> in perplexity, my perplexity may serve him.
> If I am in sorrow my sorrow may serve him.
> He does nothing in vain.
> He knows what he is about.
> He may take away my friends.
> He may throw me among strangers.
> He may make me feel desolate,
> make my spirits sink,
> hide my future from me.
> Still he knows what he is about.[112]

Jesus said to St. Maria Faustina, "The graces of My mercy are drawn by means of one vessel only, and that is trust. The more a soul trusts, the more it will receive. Souls that trust boundlessly are a great comfort to me, because I pour all the treasures of My

---

[112] John Henry Newman, *Meditations and Devotions of the Late Cardinal Newman* (N.p.: Veritatis Splendor Publications, 2012), 301.

grace into them."[113] He also told her, "Sins of distrust wound me most painfully."[114]

## What We've Learned about Suffering

It seems that all suffering is related to some sin in the world, though not necessarily that of the sufferer. The suffering and death of Christ on the Cross clearly manifests that link. As St. Paul taught, we make up in our own flesh what is lacking in the sufferings of Christ. When we suffer vicariously, we share in the mission of Christ.

As we discover in Job by the words of Elihu, God can prevent suffering, but He permits it, not only for us to make reparation for our sins but also to turn us from sin — to teach us humility and to wake us up to our sins so we will not die in them. The book of Job also teaches that suffering ultimately is a mystery.

There is much grace to be gained by accepting our suffering, even embracing it for the redemptive grace it brings. Even those who reject their suffering can, in addition to learning humility, come to realize that their fundamental option is for the world, not God. To know this clearly is a grace.

In the curing of the blind man, our Lord shows that some afflictions occur to provide Him with a situation in which to manifest His healing power. And some suffering occurs to test people and to discipline them.

Some others also seem to suffer more than their sins deserve and thus suffer vicariously. Of them we asked if, by accepting Jesus' suffering for us (which of course we must, to be saved), does

[113] Michalenko, *Mercy My Mission*, 215.
[114] *Diary*, no. 1076.

this not create a debt that our vicarious suffering could never come close to paying?

The existence of suffering calls for us to trust in God and to trust with a passion. God has shown Himself to be absolutely good, totally omnipotent, and so loving that He had His divine Son die on a Cross to make up for our sins and reconcile us to Him. I believe unequivocally that the suffering He causes or permits is 100 percent of the time to bring about a greater good; that in every case, He accomplishes with the precision of a brain surgeon some good that the elect will thank Him for eternally. He knows what He is about.

16

# "God Is Not Fair,
# So I Need Not Be Fair"

My classmate in the seminary used to say that the first thing he plans to ask God (whimsically) when he gets to heaven is, "How come *I* had to wear glasses?"

We all have questions to ask God, such as, "Why does my son have so many troubles?" or "Why did Mr. Riley have to suffer so much from cancer?" or "Why do You not strike down these evildoers?" After all, we can read in Sacred Scripture, "The arms of the wicked shall be broken, but the Lord upholds the righteous" (Ps. 37:17). Elsewhere we read:

> I will punish the world for its evil,
>   and the wicked for their iniquity;
> I will put an end to the pride of the arrogant,
>   and lay low the insolence of tyrants. (Isa. 13:11)

In Proverbs 11:21 we find:

> Be assured, the wicked will not go unpunished,
>   but those who are righteous will escape.

We sometimes wonder, "God, why are You so slow to act? People are getting away with murder!"

# Overcoming Sinful Thoughts

There is an answer in Sacred Scripture:

Because sentence against an evil deed is not executed speedily, the human heart is fully set to do evil. Though sinners do evil a hundred times and prolong their lives, yet I know that it will be well with those who fear God, because they stand in fear before him, but it will not be well with the wicked, neither will they prolong their days like a shadow, because they do not stand in fear before God. (Eccles. 8:11–13)

So, because God does not act against evildoers quickly, they pursue evil, thinking they can get away with it.

They crush your people, O LORD,
    and afflict your heritage.
They kill the widow and the stranger,
    they murder the orphan,
    and they say, "The LORD does not see;
    the God of Jacob does not perceive."

Understand, O dullest of the people;
    fools, when will you be wise?
He who planted the ear, does he not hear?
He who formed the eye, does he not see? (Ps. 94:5–9)

So we might ask, "What if God *did* punish evil right away? What would happen?" We might do good and avoid evil just to avoid punishment. It would be like the driver who is careful not to speed when a police officer is around, or near speed cameras, but drives like an Indy 500 competitor elsewhere. The speed limits on roads are ordinarily for the purpose of safety. The virtuous person keeps close to the speed limit for his safety and that of others. It comes down to prudence and love. God is looking for those virtues (and every other virtue) in us. We need every virtue to enter the kingdom.

By delaying punishment of evildoers, God insists that we grow in virtue and not just do good and avoid evil out of fear. He also indicates that justice will come for everyone, especially on Judgment Day.

What about the parable of the landowner and the workers (Matt. 20:1–16)? The landowner paid the ones who worked only one hour the same as those who worked all day. Unfair? The key to this parable is in verses 6 and 7: "And about five o'clock he went out and found others standing around; and he said to them, 'Why are you standing here idle all day?' They said to him, 'Because no one has hired us.'" In other words, they were there looking for work but had not yet been given a job. They appear to represent those who sought the truth, who sought God in whatever way they could but found Him only late in life. They will be rewarded too.

This parable might call to mind the life of St. Augustine. He sought the truth all his life, but it was only at the age of thirty-one that he found it, on hearing the voice of a child calling him to "Take and read" Sacred Scripture. There he found in Romans, "Put on the Lord Jesus Christ, and make no provision for the flesh, to gratify its desires" (Rom. 13:14). He surrendered to God late, but he was warmly welcomed by God and His Church. And how he labored for the Church with great results!

## Be Unfair!

St. Paul urges us to, in a sense, be unfair to our enemies, knowing that God will bring about justice eventually:

Bless those who persecute you; bless and do not curse them. Rejoice with those who rejoice, weep with those who weep. Live in harmony with one another; do not be haughty, but associate with the lowly; do not claim to be wiser than you are. Do not repay anyone evil for evil, but take thought for what is noble in the sight of all. If it is possible, so far as it depends on you, live peaceably with all. Beloved, never avenge yourselves, but leave room for the wrath of God; for it is written, "Vengeance is mine, I will repay, says the Lord." No, "if your enemies are hungry, feed them; if they are thirsty, give them something to drink; for by doing this you will heap burning coals on their heads." Do not be overcome by evil, but overcome evil with good. (Rom. 12:14–21)

According to St. Paul, the Christian is to *bless* his persecutors and show them kindness; feed them and give them to drink. This is certainly a new ethic, ushered in by Christ Himself. We are to overcome evil with good. How often this unconditional love has brought about peace and harmony! St. John of the Cross urges, "Where there is no love, put love, and you will take out love."

Paul is just reiterating here the teaching of Christ,

You have heard that it was said, "You shall love your neighbor and hate your enemy." But I say to you, Love your enemies and pray for those who persecute you, so that you may be children of your Father in heaven; for he makes his sun rise on the evil and on the good, and sends rain on the righteous and on the unrighteous.... Be perfect, therefore, as your heavenly Father is perfect. (Matt. 5:43–45, 48)

## God Unfair?

But there is one thing in which God was certainly not fair, and we will thank Him for it for all eternity: we sinned against God and deserved a terrible punishment, but Jesus took the punishment for us. Each of us has benefited from the sacrifice Jesus made for us and that went far beyond justice to mercy. Thank God He has not been fair with us!

I saw the following on a church's website:

> There's something about the cross that reshapes our understanding of fairness and justice. The cross was an unfair exchange. If we hold to our shallow demand for fairness, then we would see that God punished the wrong man and blessed the wrong ones. Don't misunderstand — God is just. Someone had to pay for sin and evil; it should have been us.
>
> The Gospel is completely dependent upon this unfair exchange: all of our sin for all of God's goodness. In His love, God sent His Son to provide us with the beauty of grace. We who have rebelled against God are justified because of the only man who was completely obedient to God. We who should be punished for our sins are not only unpunished but receive the gift of eternal life because Jesus, who never sinned, was brutally punished for us. While the cross was just, it was certainly not fair.[115]

We are to become like God our Father: "Be perfect, therefore, as your heavenly Father is perfect" (Matt. 5:48).

---

[115] "God's Not Fair and That's a Good Thing," NewSpring Church, https://rock.newspring.cc/articles/gods-not-fair-we-shouldnt-be-either.

17

# "I Gotta Be Free"

Freedom is defined as the power or right to act, speak, or think as one wishes without restraint. Is that a good thing? What if I want the freedom to harm, or even kill, other human beings? Or to take advantage of a friend? What if I use my freedom to rob banks or to commit any other crime?

Freedom for a Christian is something quite different from worldly sin. It is the power to do what we ought, the power to love God and neighbor and never act against that love. It is the power to live a life of virtue, to make a habit of doing what is good. That implies all sorts of constraints, the kind of constraints that God Himself has: He may not lie; He may not do any kind of evil. If He did, He would no longer be good; but God is by definition good.

The Latin word for *free* is *liber*. But there is another definition of the word *liber*: "alone." If you are completely free of any constraints in your life, you will be alone. You will have no friends, because friendship implies a certain accommodation toward our friends. If your friend is allergic to cigar smoke, you should avoid smoking cigars in her presence. Love brings constraints. There is no way around that.

Archbishop Sheen wrote, "The evil behind the devil's question in the garden was God cannot be good if he does not let you do whatever you please. Freedom to Satan is the absence from law and constraint. The unconverted believed that freedom was the right to do whatever you *pleased* rather than the right to do whatever you *ought*."[116]

St. John Paul II said something similar:

> Every generation of Americans needs to know that freedom consists not in doing what we like, but in having the right to do what we ought.... We must guard the truth that is the condition of authentic freedom, the truth that allows freedom to be fulfilled in goodness.
>
> We must guard the deposit of divine truth handed down to us in the Church, especially in view of the challenges posed by a materialistic culture and by a permissive mentality that reduces freedom to license."[117]

Elsewhere St. John Paul II proclaimed:

> True freedom is not advanced in the permissive society, which confuses freedom with license to do anything whatever and which in the name of freedom proclaims a kind of general amorality. It is a caricature of freedom to claim that people are free to organize their lives with no reference to moral values, and to say that society does not have to ensure the protection and advancement of ethical values. Such an attitude is destructive of freedom and peace."[118]

---

[116] Fulton J. Sheen, *Preface to Religion* (Martino Fine Books, 2017), 48–49.
[117] Pope John Paul II, Homily at Mass, Oriole Park at Camden Yards, Baltimore (October 8, 1995).
[118] Pope John Paul II, Message for the World Day of Peace (January 1, 1981), no. 7.

St. Augustine wrote, "The good man, though a slave, is free; the wicked, though he reigns, is a slave, and not the slave of a single man, but—what is worse—the slave of as many masters as he has vices."[119] In saying this he was just elaborating on the words of Christ:

> Then Jesus said to the Jews who had believed in him, "If you continue in my word, you are truly my disciples; and you will know the truth, and the truth will make you free." They answered him, "We are descendants of Abraham and have never been slaves to anyone. What do you mean by saying, 'You will be made free'? Jesus answered them, "Very truly, I tell you, everyone who commits sin is a slave to sin." (John 8:31–35)

Benjamin Franklin asserted that "only a virtuous people are capable of freedom. As nations become corrupt and vicious, they have more need of masters."

Being bound by the truth, bound to a spouse, bound to children, bound to others in friendship, bound to virtue, bound to the common good—these are the best ways to exercise freedom. Above all is being bound to God. (*Religare*, from which Latin word comes the word *religion*, means to bind.) These are the choices that fulfill us and make us happy in the end.

∞

So if, by *freedom*, we mean being able to do whatever we want, without restraint, we should realize the folly of such a power. It will isolate us from God, our family, and our neighbors. If, by *freedom*, we mean being able to do what we ought, and what binds us to God and others in love, we should seek it and promote it everywhere.

[119] St. Augustine, *City of God*, bk. 4, chap. 3.

18

# "I Can Find Heaven on Earth"

The person who says, "I can find heaven on earth" usually means he hopes to find happiness by the accumulation of riches. Although it seems that few people actually make that statement, a good number live as if that were their goal.

The fictional play *Doctor Faustus* portrays a man who proposes a pact with the devil to sell his soul in exchange for twenty-four years of power to do whatever he wants. After vacillating back and forth, he signs the contract in his blood. After the twenty-four years are up, he must surrender his soul for all eternity. The point of the play is that he made a bad bargain (clearly!). To a degree, all of us may be tempted to sell our souls—or a part thereof—to the devil for power or success.

We might think there are few instances of that happening today, but it happens in politics quite often. Politicians who claim to be Christians will become "pro-choice" (pro-abortion "rights"), or embrace a position favoring same-sex "marriage" so as to get elected, despite biblical principles against these things.[120]

---

[120] And yet we must never write these persons off and assume they will be lost. We are obliged to pray for them and pray hard. We want them to reform and to be with us in the kingdom.

Another example might be the person who refuses to help the poor, using all his wealth for himself. A related aspect of this building heaven on earth is seeking happiness through wealth or possessions. Jesus warned against this: "Do not store up for yourselves treasures on earth, where moth and rust consume and where thieves break in and steal; but store up for yourselves treasures in heaven, where neither moth nor rust consumes and where thieves do not break in and steal. For where your treasure is, there your heart will be also" (Matt. 6:19–20). And again: "For what will it profit them to gain the whole world and forfeit their life? Indeed, what can they give in return for their life?" (Mark 8:36–37).

In an article published in 2017, researchers found that millionaires are generally happier than those with a net worth below that level. Those with a net worth of over ten million dollars are just slightly happier than those who have only (!) a million. Those who earned their millions are happier than those who inherited it. The researchers found that those who earned $100,000 a year were not much happier than those who made $75,000 a year. Those conducting the study found that those who gave away much of their fortunes found more happiness than those who spent them on themselves.[121]

A different study in 2017 found that wealthy people tended to be more self-centered than those who were less affluent. The researchers compared the financial situation of each participant against how often they felt the emotions awe, compassion,

---

[121] Peter Cohan, "This Harvard Study of 4,000 Millionaires Revealed Something Surprising about Money and Happiness," *Inc.*, December 14, 2017, https://www.inc.com/peter-cohan/will-10-million-make-you-happier-harvard-says-yes-if-you-make-it-yourself-give-it-away.html.

contentment, enthusiasm, love, and pride. The study, published by the American Psychological Association, found that "people with lower incomes find happiness in other people, through feelings of love and compassion, according to new research. However, rich people find their happiness in more self-involved traits, such as pride." Those who are less affluent had emotions relating to other people, especially compassion and love. They also were more likely to feel awe and beauty relating to their environment. The authors of the study wrote, "Lower-income individuals have devised a way to cope, to find meaning, joy and happiness in their lives despite their relatively less favorable circumstances." The less affluent find fulfillment in deeper elements of life.[122]

Another study, appearing in 2018 in the journal *Nature Human Behavior*, found that the wealthier we become, beyond a certain point, the less happy we are. The researchers found that earning more than $105,000 per year in the United States (or $95,000 globally) "tended to be associated with reduced life satisfaction and a lower level of well-being." And the same applied to children in families with these income levels.[123]

So what is the problem? According to the Purdue University researchers conducting the 2018 study, it seems that once you have enough money to fulfill your fundamental needs, more

[122] Sarah Young, "Being Rich Makes You More Selfish, Finds Study," *Independent*, December 18, 2017, https://www.independent.co.uk/life-style/rich-selfish-higher-incomes-happiness-self-centered-emotion-american-psychological-association-a8116846.html.

[123] Catey Hill, "The Dark Reasons So Many Rich People Are Miserable Human Beings," MarketWatch, February 22, 2018, https://www.marketwatch.com/story/the-dark-reasons-so-many-rich-people-are-miserable-human-beings-2018-02-22.

money may lead to pursuing additional material possessions and making comparisons with the affluence of others. Both of these tend to decrease our personal fulfillment.

> The problem … of course, is that plenty of research shows that most material possessions don't make us happier — instead, it's things like experiences and having more time to do things we love — and spend time with people we love — that drive happiness. "The deepest pleasures are derived from interpersonal love, warm relationships, giving, appreciation, and gratitude," explains Fran Walfish, a Beverly Hills family and relationship psychotherapist and author of "The Self-Aware Parent."[124]

There is another problem with increasing income immoderately: it tends to move us away from others, to isolation. This could result from selfishness or competition. Or it might just be that with affluence we don't need others as much as we did when we were less affluent. In any case, being less associated with others reduces our sense of well-being. A further problem for some high-earners is that such people tend to become workaholics. The *Atlantic* magazine pointed out that wealthy men in the United States work longer hours than those who are less wealthy and longer hours than the rich in other countries. They have less leisure time than the others. It is that leisure time to be with family and friends that tends to make us happy.[125]

So, if we hope to find a "heaven on earth" through wealth and possessions, we are barking up the wrong tree. As the psalmist wrote:

[124] Hill, "Dark Reasons."
[125] Hill, "Dark Reasons."

Like sheep they are appointed for Sheol;
　　Death shall be their shepherd;
straight to the grave they descend,
　　and their form shall waste away;
　　Sheol shall be their home.
But God will ransom my soul from the power of Sheol,
　　for he will receive me.

Do not be afraid when some become rich,
　　when the wealth of their houses increases.
For when they die they will carry nothing away;
　　their wealth will not go down after them.
Though in their lifetime they count themselves happy
　　—for you are praised when you do well for yourself—
they will go to the company of their ancestors,
　　who will never again see the light.
Mortals cannot abide in their pomp;
　　they are like the animals that perish. (Ps. 49:14–21)

∞

So pursuing riches hoping for happiness is foolish. There is nothing wrong with seeking happiness in this world, especially if we seek it in the Lord. The psalmists tell us: "Take delight in the Lord, and he will give you the desires of your heart" (Ps. 37:4); "O taste and see that the Lord is good; happy are those who take refuge in him!" (Ps. 34:8); and "Happy are the people whose God is the Lord!" (Ps. 144:15). But we must always remember that no matter how rich a person might become, he won't find in his wealth a happiness that could be even close to the happiness of heaven. In this life, there will always be suffering and death, but these will not exist in the eternal kingdom:

Then I saw a new heaven and a new earth; for the first heaven and the first earth had passed away, and the sea was no more. And I saw the holy city, the new Jerusalem, coming down out of heaven from God, prepared as a bride adorned for her husband. And I heard a loud voice from the throne saying,

"See, the home of God is among mortals.
He will dwell with them;
they will be his peoples,
and God himself will be with them;
he will wipe every tear from their eyes.
Death will be no more;
mourning and crying and pain will be no more,
for the first things have passed away." (Rev. 21:1–4)

That is the heaven we should strive for, the everlasting heaven.

19

# "Nothing Can Help Me Break
That Sinful Habit"

St. Camillus de Lellis was born in 1550 to a timid mother and a shiftless father. His father worked as a soldier for hire in any army that would pay him, regardless of its cause. He seems to have embraced all the typical vices of his military peers, including spending money frivolously and gambling endlessly.

Camillus had a wild temper, like his father. He pursued a dysfunctional life from an early age and became addicted to gambling. The one thing he gained from his devout mother, who died when he was just twelve, was a deep respect for religion.

At age seventeen, he joined his father and became with him a professional gambler. His wild temper gained him the reputation of being, like his father, constantly ready for a fight. Once, while on their way to join an army, both became quite ill. As his father neared death, Camillus was impressed when he repented of his sins and devoutly received the last sacraments. He died shortly thereafter. As a result, Camillus took stock of his sinful life and resolved to enter a monastery and reform his life. When he applied to the Franciscans he was treated well, but they could not accept him as a religious.

# Overcoming Sinful Thoughts

He wandered to Rome, where he sought to work in a hospital as a servant in return for treatment for a long-festering sore on his leg. He started out well there but soon returned to his gambling and fighting ways. So he was fired and sent away.

He went back to being a soldier for hire, fighting for the Venice army. He fought well for Venice, but, unfortunately, he could not tame his fighting, and he was fired.

One day, at age twenty-four, he was begging outside a church when a wealthy man approached him and offered him a job to help build a monastery. Camillus agreed.

He threw himself into the job, knowing it might be the hardest thing he had ever attempted. The hard work, the daily grind with no adventure, and the taunts of the children pushed him to the brink. But he kept on. He had to keep in check his gambling addiction and his temper, and he did.

In time, his leg wound worsened, so he went to Rome to work in a hospital and get medical help. He loved serving the sick, but he soon found that they were treated badly by the nurses *and* the priests. So he started a group of nurses to serve the sick out of love. Then he studied for the priesthood and was ordained at age thirty-four. His hospital work began to thrive, as did his spiritual life. He revolutionized health care and is considered the father of modern nursing.

The point of all this is that Camillus is an example of a saint who struggled and fell again and again, but finally, with the help of God and others, he triumphed over his shameful past and gave himself entirely over to the Lord and his brothers and sisters in need. St. Paul, St. Augustine, and St. Margaret of Cortona had rather sudden conversions and stayed on track thereafter. St. Camillus fell and got up again, and the world is so much better for it.

When a sinner keeps falling and getting up again, he should keep in mind the words of our Savior: "The Son of Man came to seek out and to save the lost" (Luke 19:10). He should also remember Jesus' great concern for sinners:

> Then Levi [also known as St. Matthew] gave a great banquet for [Jesus] in his house; and there was a large crowd of tax collectors and others sitting at the table with them. The Pharisees and their scribes were complaining to his disciples, saying, "Why do you eat and drink with tax collectors and sinners?" Jesus answered, "Those who are well have no need of a physician, but those who are sick; I have come to call not the righteous but sinners to repentance." (Luke 5:29–32)

Also, our Lord proclaims, "I tell you, there will be more joy in heaven over one sinner who repents than over ninety-nine righteous persons who need no repentance" (Luke 15:7). It should be clear from all this that Jesus takes a special interest in sinners and helping them reform. He was even more explicit about this in his private revelation to St. Maria Faustina, where he told her, "The greater the sinner, the greater the right he has to My mercy."[126]

There are many addictions that people deal with, including smoking and excessive drinking. It is estimated that smokers, on average, make anywhere from eight to thirty attempts to quit before they finally give up smoking for a year.[127] Among those

---

[126] *Diary*, no. 723.

[127] "Quitting Smoking? Expect a Lot of Failure before You Succeed" Healthline, https://www.healthline.com/health-news/quitting-smoking-expect-failure-before-you-succeed#1.

trying to overcome alcoholism, studies indicate that 80 percent of those who try to stop drinking have at least one relapse before they conquer the addiction.[128] But about one in three do achieve full recovery.[129] Groups such as AA provide excellent support for those trying to conquer their habit.

So, there is hope for all those caught up in addictive behavior, and support groups can be a wonderful help in reform.[130] And every Christian should remember the saying quoted in chapter 6: the difference between a saint and sinner is this: a saint is a sinner who never stopped trying.

---

[130] For further reading, see Fr. Richard Heilman, "Twelve Things to Remember if You Keep Falling into the Same Sin," Roman Catholic Man, February 13, 2015, https://www.romancatholic-man.com/twelve-things-to-remember-if-you-keep-falling-into-the-same-sin/.

20

# "I Don't Have to Love My Enemies Because They Are Clearly Doing Evil"

We need not like our enemies, that's for sure. If we liked them, they wouldn't be our enemies. But loving them is another issue. Unfortunately, in the English language, *love* is often used as the superlative of *like*. I love my new car; I love that movie; I love football. In a Christian context, however, *love* means something entirely different. When our blessed Lord says we must love our neighbor as ourselves, He uses the Greek word *agapao*. A good definition for *agapao* (or, in noun form, *agape*) would be "a giving of self for the good of the beloved without conditions."

So this love is something we *will*, not something we *feel*. In essence, to say "I love you" in this context means "I will work for your good no matter what happens." This is how God loves us. He is always sending us help to overcome our sins and live in an intimate, warm relationship with Him.

God commands us to love our neighbor as ourselves. That means we are concerned for our neighbor's good as much as we are concerned for our own good. But does God command us to love our enemies? He certainly does:

# Overcoming Sinful Thoughts

> You have heard that it was said, "You shall love your neighbor and hate your enemy." But I say to you, Love your enemies and pray for those who persecute you, so that you may be children of your Father who is in heaven; for he makes his sun rise on the evil and on the good, and sends rain on the righteous and on the unrighteous. For if you love those who love you, what reward do you have? Do not even the tax collectors do the same? And if you greet only your brothers and sisters, what more are you doing than others? Do not even the Gentiles do the same? Be perfect, therefore, as your heavenly Father is perfect. (Matt. 5:43–48)

So we might infer that loving our enemy is a part of the Christian perfection to which we are all called.

Some of the saints — and other good people — provide us with great examples of loving their enemies. Once, one of Francis de Sales's priests became angry when he was turned down for a position that was beyond his capabilities. In response, the priest published a pamphlet ridiculing Francis and had the nerve to hand a copy of it to him in person while he was leading a religious event at the cathedral. The bishop read it and did nothing about it. Later, instead of penalizing the priest, as his friends suggested, he treated him kindly and even granted him favors.

In 2016, when ISIS had been driven out of Fallujah, a group of volunteers approached a detainment camp containing a number of ISIS members. They provided them food and comfort, knowing that the ones they were serving were convicted ISIS members. The leader of the group, a Muslim named Sadiq, recognized an ISIS member and told him, "You killed my friend. But I've come here to feed you." The team of volunteers thought they would receive a hostile reception, but instead they found row after row of broken men. They broke down in tears, saying "I'm sorry, I'm sorry, I'm sorry."

The lead editor of the humanitarian group, Matthew Willingham, a Christian, commented on the encounter, "I see this as the love of God reaching down into the world.... That's a Christ-like love extended to [Sadiq's] enemies. Not people he disagrees with, but his enemies. People who murdered his friends. That is the love of God in Christ. Love has the power to convict." He wrote that he saw the love of Christ that day, in Sadiq, a Muslim.[131]

"If your enemies are hungry, give them bread to eat; and if they are thirsty, give them water to drink" (Prov. 25:21).

[131] Carey Lodge, "Meet the Christians Who Love Their Enemies, Even When It's ISIS," *Christian Today*, September 14, 2016, https://www.christiantoday.com/article/meet.the.christians.who. love.their.enemies.even.when.its.isis/95436.htm.

# 21

# "I Can't Help Acting on My Temptations, So I'm Not to Blame"

Long before I entered the seminary, I was talking to a young woman and asked about her prayer life. She told me, "I have to overcome some of my sins before I go to God in prayer." I told her she had it backward. We go to God in prayer even while sinners, to seek the strength to overcome our sins.

To deny that we can overcome our temptations is to deny our freedom. But we all have a certain amount of freedom. The *Catechism of the Catholic Church* teaches, "As long as freedom has not bound itself definitively to its ultimate good which is God, there is the possibility of choosing between good and evil, and thus of growing in perfection or of failing and sinning. This freedom characterizes properly human acts. It is the basis of praise or blame, merit or reproach" (1732).

In order to exercise freedom, we must make progress in "virtue, knowledge of the good, and ascesis (self-denial)" (1734). Granted, our responsibility can be reduced under certain conditions: "Imputability and responsibility for an action can be diminished or even nullified by ignorance, inadvertence, duress, fear, habit, inordinate attachments, and other psychological or social factors" (1735).

Still, "every act directly willed is imputable to its author" (1736). It seems that even if our freedom is diminished by fear, habit, and so forth, we all have some degree of freedom. And, we all have freedom to discover which acts are wrong and get the help we need to overcome them. In other words, there is just about always a way to seek the help of others — through counseling, substance-abuse programs, and various support groups — and above all to seek God's grace through prayer and the sacraments. A proper approach is to "pray as if everything depends on God, and work as if everything depends on us."

Sacred Scripture affords us hope in our struggle against sin: "If we confess our sins, he who is faithful and just will forgive us our sins and purify us from all unrighteousness" (1 John 1:9). And, "I can do all things through him [Christ] who strengthens me" (Phil. 4:13). Finally, "No testing has overtaken you that is not common to everyone. God is faithful, and he will not let you be tested beyond your strength, but with the testing he will also provide the way out so that you may be able to endure it" (1 Cor. 10:13).

Sometimes we must pray very hard to overcome a life of sin. Many sinners have sought the intercession of the Blessed Virgin Mary to cease their sins, with great results.

The story is told of an Augustinian sister who had a regular practice of praying for those who died in her town. In the same town lived a terrible sinner named Mary, who had been expelled from the community. She lived in a cave outside the town and died seemingly in a state of sin, as an outcast, without the benefit of receiving any sacraments. She was buried in a field, like an animal.

When Sr. Catherine heard of Mary's death, she assumed the poor woman was in hell and didn't bother to pray for her. After about four years, a soul from purgatory appeared to Sr. Catherine and lamented, "Sr. Catherine, I am so unhappy. You pray for all the souls who have died, but not for me."

"Who are you?" asked Sr. Catherine.

"I am that miserable Mary who died in my cave."

"How can this be? Are you saved?" asked Sr. Catherine.

"Yes, I am saved," answered Mary, "by the mercy of the Blessed Virgin Mary."

"But how?" asked Sr. Catherine.

"When I saw my death approaching, weighed down by my innumerable sins and rejected by everyone, I turned to Blessed Mary and prayed, 'O sweet Mother, you are the hope of sinners; look at me in my final hours, totally abandoned. You are my only hope; you alone can help. I beg you have pity on me.' The Virgin Mary obtained for me the grace of saying an act of contrition before I died. My Queen also acquired for me the grace that my pains should be more intense and thus shortened. Otherwise they would have lasted many years. Just a few Masses are required to end my stay in Purgatory. Please have them offered for me, and I promise to pray for you."

Sr. Catherine arranged for those Masses to be said for her and Mary appeared to her just days later radiating a bright light and said, "Thank you, Sr. Catherine. I am now on my way to heaven to thank God for His mercy and to pray for you."

Another account of the Virgin Mary's extraordinary intercession for a sinner occurred in the nineteenth century. A widow who had lost her husband to suicide went to see St. John Vianney in Ars, France. As he walked by her waiting in line to see him, he stopped and, though he had never seen her before, looked at her and told her, "He is saved! He is in purgatory.... Between the bridge and the water he had time to make an act of contrition.

Our Blessed Lady obtained that grace for him. . . . Though he had no religion he sometimes prayed the Marian prayers with you in May. This merited him the grace of repentance."

Everyone mired in sin should call on Mary. She has a long list of sinners whom she has helped to receive God's endless mercy.

The Church has a long list of those who were great and constant sinners who, by God's grace, were able to reform and become holy: Bl. Bartolo Longo (Satanist priest); St. Angela Foligno (adulteress); St. Margaret of Cortona (mistress); St. Camillus (rabble rouser; see chapter 19); St. Mary Magdalene (possessed by seven devils).

God's mercy is available to anyone who asks for it, especially through the intercession of the Blessed Virgin Mary.

22

# "I Will Do Anything to Avoid Loneliness"

Psychologist John Cacioppo of the University of Chicago performed a number of studies on loneliness. The first thing he discovered was that doctors reported that they were able to provide better medical care to patients whose families are supportive and who are socially connected. Those who are lonely indicate they have higher levels of stress when dealing with the same stressful situations as the non-lonely, even in times of relaxation.

Being very lonely increases stress hormones and blood pressure. It hinders regulation of the circulatory system, causing the heart to work harder. It also diminishes sleep efficiency, reducing its restorative benefits. "Loneliness," Cacioppo concluded, "sets in motion a variety of 'slowly unfolding pathophysiological processes.' The net result is that the lonely experience higher levels of cumulative wear and tear."[132]

A recent study has shown that our social media culture, including Facebook, Twitter, and other web-based networks,

---

[132] Hara Estroff Marano, "The Dangers of Loneliness," *Psychology Today*, July 1, 2003, https://www.psychologytoday.com/us/articles/200307/the-dangers-loneliness.

are fostering more loneliness. Nearly half the Americans polled reported they felt alone, isolated, or left out at various times. "The nation's 75 million millennials (ages 23 to 37) and Generation Z adults (18 to 22) are lonelier than any other U.S. demographic and report being in worse health than older generations."[133]

It seems that everyone feels lonely from time to time, especially after losing a family member or ending a romantic relationship. But chronic loneliness is rarer and more serious.

How does a person overcome loneliness? Some of the ways people try to rid themselves of the feeling of loneliness are counterproductive and sinful: drinking excessively, taking recreational drugs, or pursuing illicit sexual relationships, either heterosexual or same-sex.

Arthur H. Brand, Ph.D., a licensed psychologist in Boca Raton, Florida, suggests that the best way to overcome loneliness is to have face-to-face involvement with others—for example: "support groups, civic activities, adult education classes, social groups, volunteering, faith-based activities, political activism, book clubs, travel clubs, and even dating web sites."[134]

Other things that can help are getting the right amount of sleep, working normal hours, connecting often with family members and getting regular exercise. Author Jennifer Page has written a book about overcoming loneliness. Some of her ideas include the following:

---

[133] Nick Tate, "Loneliness Rivals Obesity, Smoking as Health Risk," WebMD, May 4, 2018, https://www.webmd.com/balance/news/20180504/loneliness-rivals-obesity-smoking-as-health-risk.
[134] Tate, "Loneliness Rivals Obesity."

1. Make the effort to form friendships, and put time into friendships to make them deeper. And, to be sure, connecting with God would be the first thing to pursue.
2. Be real. Be yourself. Of course, you must discover yourself first.
3. Don't just sit there, do things! Do the things you've been putting off for twenty minutes a day.
4. Turn off the TV. Studies have shown that those who watch too much TV have a lower amount of life satisfaction.
5. Write something daily, in a journal or whatever. And read something daily.
6. Enjoy solitude.
7. Thank God every day for your blessings.[135]

∽

Some degree of loneliness is normal and not to be feared. When it becomes burdensome, there are plenty of legitimate, innocent ways to address it. There's no reason to fall into sinful behavior in a desperate attempt to escape being lonely.

---

[135] Jennifer Page, *Freedom from Loneliness: 52 Ways to Stop Feeling Lonely* (self-pub., 2012).

23

# "My Life Is Hard;
# I Deserve Some 'Compensation'
# (A Little Sin Now and Then)"

When you are stressed by your daily life, you often *do* need a break. The key is to pursue breaks that are not sinful. The world offers so many opportunities to indulge ourselves, some sinful, some not. Well, I admit, *many* sinful. I suppose behind many such statements as this chapter's title is the feeling, "I have abstained from many sinful indulgences for so long. I feel so boxed in that I need some outlet."

This, of course, is a mistaken view of the life of virtue. The foundational moral virtue is prudence, which makes a habit of acting reasonably, or, as St. Thomas Aquinas put it, according to right reason. The worldly see that as quite constraining, being contrary to our human nature.

But, in fact, acting reasonably is the fulfillment of our human nature; it is in keeping with our dignity as human beings, created in the image and likeness of God. And we should remember that not every indulgence is sinful. There is nothing wrong with watching a good, decent movie, drinking a glass of wine, consuming a healthy meal, taking a warm bath, or listening to some Mozart. The demonic wants us to believe that only sinful indulgences will give us joy. And while we are at it, we should remind ourselves that not every pleasure is evil. As Aristotle taught, pleasure is good if it accompanies a (morally) good action; evil if it accompanies a (morally) evil action.

No one ever found a lasting, fulfilling happiness through sinful pleasures. St. Augustine tried it and found it wanting. He wrote:

> Late have I loved you, O Beauty so ancient and so new.... I rushed headlong after these things of beauty which you have made.... They kept me far from you, those fair things which, were they not in you, would not exist at all.... You have sent forth fragrance, and I have drawn in my breath, and I pant for you. I have tasted you, and I hunger and thirst for you. You have touched me and I have burned for your peace.[136]

Augustine tasted the illicit delights of this world and was perceptive enough to realize they didn't satisfy. After just a taste of heaven, experienced through prayer and fasting, he realized that all beauty, all joys of this world, are just a whisper of the beauty and joy to be found in God, in this life and in the life to come. That is the first task of every Christian, of every person: to discover the unfathomable glory of being united with God, now and forever.

So enjoy, indulge on occasion and at the right time, but there is no need to sin. For example, how many people of faith will watch a movie with lots of sex and violence, when there are any number of decent alternatives?

---

[136] *The Confessions of St. Augustine*, bk 10, chap. 27. This quote is an adaptation from that found in the translation by John K. Ryan (New York: Image Books, 1960), 254–255.

## Sinless Entertainment

### Movies

To name just a few, here are some Christian movies that are *very* entertaining:

- *Fireproof*, a well-written movie on how a man saved his marriage from disaster with help from his father
- *Facing the Giants*, an inspiring movie about a team that was floundering and then began to win when the coach got them to play for Christ
- *Courageous*, in which a group of men get together to live their manhood for God
- *War Room*, about a woman and her "war room" (place of prayer)[137]
- *God's Not Dead*, in which an arrogant agnostic college professor challenges a student to disprove his statement that God is dead (There are two more *God's Not Dead* movies, which are equally entertaining and promote Christian themes.)
- *The Case for Christ*, in which an atheist decides he will research Christianity to show his Christian wife that it makes no sense and, in the process, becomes a believer himself (Be sure to watch the drama, not the documentary.)

Virtually all good Christian movies can be streamed for under four dollars each at Christian Cinema (no subscription needed).

---

[137] *Fireproof, Facing the Giants, Courageous,* and *War Room* were produced by the Kendrick brothers and the members of a Baptist church in Albany, Georgia. Other films they've produced include *Flywheel* and their most recent one, *Overcomer*.

*Books*

Some very interesting books that promote Christianity and decency include biographies of saints:

- *Treasure in Clay*, the autobiography of Bishop Fulton Sheen
- *Our Lady of Guadalupe*, by William Carroll
- *America's Bishop*, by Thomas Reeves, a biography of Bishop Sheen, which covers the negative as well as the positive (overall, quite positive)
- *Fatima in Brief*, a book I wrote to get the Fatima message out (only 100 pages, so there's no fluff in it)
- *St. Francis of Assisi*, by Léopold de Chérancé — the best book on St. Francis (out of print, but can be downloaded at Free Traditional Catholic Books, https://www.traditionalcatholic.co/free-catholicbooks/)
- *A Tuscan Penitent: The Life and Legend of St. Margaret of Cortona*, by Father Cuthbert — an excellent, fascinating account of this beautiful, reformed sinner
- *Mercy My Mission: Life of Sister Faustina H. Kowalska* (1987), by Sister Sophia Michalenko — a great account of St. Maria Faustina and the Divine Mercy Devotion

And some books on extraordinary conversions:

- *The Case for Christ*, by Lee Strobel (see the movie above)
- *Forever Young*, by Joan Wester Anderson — a biography of Catholic movie star Loretta Young
- *Of Men and Mary*, by Christine Watkins — one of the most inspiring books I have ever read
- *Full of Grace*, by Christine Watkins — another collection of inspiring conversions

These titles were chosen because they are *very* interesting. Sometimes when you are stressed you are not up for reading a book, but these books become very entertaining just a few pages in. The words seem to jump off the pages!

You can find hundreds of books on the saints to download for free at Free Traditional Catholic Books, www.traditionalcatholic. co/free-catholicbooks/. Or enter "free download saints books" in a search engine.

### Music

Listening to classical (or other) music can be very relaxing. You can download a large number of classical works by Mozart, Bach, Beethoven, and other greats for free at www.classicalcat.net and https://musopen.org/music/. There are several other websites that provide free downloads of classical music MP3 files as well. To see the best five of these, go to https://www.lifewire.com/free-classical-music-downloads-1358036. I downloaded a number of these some years back, put them on a CD, and have been playing them in my car ever since. Great stuff!

### Sports

There are any number of sports clips on Youtube and other video streaming sites. You can watch whole football games, highlights, tennis matches, basketball games, and much more, all at no cost.

∞

Some believe, as the famous quote attributed to Saint Louis businessman Frank Rand put it, "It seems as if anything I like is either illegal, immoral, or fattening." It just isn't so. You may have to look a bit harder to find them, but there are *many* alternatives to things "illegal, immoral or fattening." Christians and non-Christians alike should make the effort to find them. Sin is never harmless. It harms the sinner first and drags the whole world down a notch. And, of course, it draws us away from our first love, God.

So, take a break when you need one, and enjoy yourself. But you need not sin when you do.

# 24

# "My Way or the Highway"

Years back, I worked with a young man who was engaged to be married. He was entertaining doubts about the marriage. His fiancée seemed to be controlling at times. So I suggested that he postpone the wedding. He proposed that to his fiancée, and her initial reaction was, "We either go with our wedding date, or we don't get married." Control at its finest!

He stuck to his guns and insisted on the postponement. Psychologists recommend that when faced with a manipulative encounter, you say something like, "Well, that's what I'm going to do. It's your decision as to what you will do as a result." That's essentially what this young man said, and in a few days, his fiancée decided to live with the postponement. However, once he had stepped back from the commitment, he realized he didn't want to deal with her manipulative ways, and he broke off the relationship.

He later met a good Catholic at an online dating site and ended up marrying her. He told me she was the most delightful woman he ever dated and was so happy that I had helped him to see the mistake he was about to make with the other woman.

Manipulation is forcing others to do what they don't want to do. Conversion is helping others to see the benefits of doing what they thought they didn't want to do, or what they never thought of doing, and doing it happily.

Some people use anger as a manipulative tool. Every time they don't get what they want, they explode in anger. They hope others will comply with their demands for fear of having to deal with their wrath.

Marriage books often caution wives about pushing too hard for their husbands to attend Mass or go to Confession or pray. Husbands have a tendency to push back when they feel their wives are trying to control them. Counselors encourage wives to be very gentle in encouraging religious participation by their husbands, saying things like, "I am going to Mass now. Let me know if you would like to come with me," rather than, "You need to go to Mass today."

Granted, a man should be beyond pushing back over his wife's suggestions, especially on religious practices, but not all men are. It's best not to nag, regardless. *Nagging* is another word for *manipulating*. It's important to honor a person's freedom, even if we think he is misusing that freedom.

This applies to parents regarding their adult children's religious practices. I encourage parents to tell them, "I required you to come to Mass and pray often just as I required you to go to school. Just as requiring school wouldn't guarantee that you would become a scholar, neither would having you attend Mass and pray guarantee that you would come to love God. But my duty as a parent was to give you the knowledge to know how to become a scholar or to love God. No one can force you to do either one of these things. You're a free agent. Loving God is up to you. I can't do that for you." Of course, an adult child living at home should follow the house rules, especially if there are younger children living at home.

A woman who was into health food tried to get her husband to eat her health food as well. She kept nagging him, and he always refused, and finally he began to smoke and drink. Another woman started on health food and asked her husband if he would mind if she prepared health food for herself and regular food for him. He agreed. After a year, he began to eat health food with her. Very different approaches, very different results.

When we plan an event, such as a party or a prayer meeting, and people opt out, we may feel like we'd like to make them come, or feel bad that they didn't come. That's a manipulative instinct. We need to get rid of such thoughts fast. If a person opts out of something, we should tell ourselves, "So they didn't make it. That's life. Move on."

A young man was invited to a spiritual talk by an acquaintance, and he replied, "I'm sorry, I won't be able to make it." The inviting party responded, "I will tell God." The invited person replied, "Get over it." Classic attempt at control, and the response was not surprising.

So it's important for us to realize that manipulation or control is an attempt to override the freedom of others. As Christians, we should honor others' freedom.

25

# "Going to Confession Is Too Embarrassing; I Don't Remember How; It's Easier Not to Go"

To confess our sins to a priest is difficult at times. It can be shameful as well. But it is enriching because it is an encounter with our all-loving, all-merciful God.

Uncertainty about the details of the sacrament should not be a concern. In generations past, priests expected penitents to know how to confess and to have memorized the Act of Contrition as well. Not anymore. Most Catholic schoolchildren learn to begin, "Bless me, Father, for I have sinned," but a fair number of people—young and old—come in and say nothing and are clearly not familiar with the process. So we priests begin for them, "In the name of the Father, and of the Son.... How long has it been since your last confession?" Once they answer, we may ask "Now, what are your sins?"

Once they have told us their sins (only mortal sins must be confessed by type and approximate number), we give them a penance and ask them if they know the Act of Contrition. If not, we usually have copies of that prayer available right in front of them for them to read. In cases where, for some reason, we don't have the Act of Contrition available, we offer to lead them through it. Easy.

What if it has been a year, or five years, or twenty years since they confessed? We don't yell at them. We often say, "Welcome back. I have been waiting for you."

## Direct Confession

There are any number of other excuses, besides the above, for not confessing. One of the most popular excuses for not going to Confession is "I don't need to go to a priest. I can confess directly to God." St. Augustine had to deal with this in the fifth century: "Let no one say, I do penance secretly; I perform it in the sight of God, and He who is to pardon me knows that in my heart I repent.... Was it then said to no purpose, 'What you shall loose upon earth shall be loosed in heaven'? Was it for nothing that the keys were given to the Church?"[138]

## Serious Sins

You can indeed confess directly to God and be forgiven venial sins. However, as the *Catechism of the Catholic Church* teaches, "Individual and integral confession of grave sins followed by absolution remains the only ordinary means of reconciliation with God and with the Church" (1497). For mortal sins we need more than just "direct confession." Anyone conscious of grave sin must receive the sacrament of Reconciliation before going to Communion (1385).

---

[138] St. Augustine, sermon 392, as quoted in Edward Hanna, "The Sacrament of Penance," *Catholic Encyclopedia* (New York: Robert Appleton, 1911), http://www.newadvent.org/cathen/11618c.htm.

## Amazing Grace

By not making use of the sacrament of Reconciliation, you do not receive the sacramental grace that is available there. St. Francis de Sales wrote:

> In confession you not only receive absolution from the ... sins you confess, but also great strength to avoid them in the future, light to see them clearly, and abundant grace to repair whatever damage you have incurred. You will also practice the virtues of humility, obedience, simplicity, and charity. In the single act of confession you will exercise more virtues than in any other act whatsoever.[139]

St. John Vianney said, "When you go to confession you must understand ... you are about to un-nail Our Lord."[140] And St. Dorotheus insisted on the importance of identifying and confessing our failings as we strive for holiness: "It does not matter how many virtues a man may have, even if they are beyond number and limit. If he has turned from the path of self-accusation, he will never find peace."[141]

## Confirmation and Counsel

When you confess directly to God, you don't hear the words of absolution from the priest, by which you can be sure you have

---

[139] St. Francis de Sales, *Introduction to the Devout Life*, trans. John K. Ryan (New York: Image Books, 1972), 111–112.

[140] Quoted in George William Rutler, *The Curé of Ars Today* (San Francisco: Ignatius Press, 1988), 153.

[141] "Teachings of St. Dorotheas, Abbot," in *Liturgy of the Hours*, Office of Readings, Monday of Week 9 in Ordinary Time.

been forgiven. Jesus gave His apostles the power to forgive *and retain* sins.[142] A priest can often tell if you are truly contrite for your sins. He can help you know what things are truly wrong and what things are serious matter. It is said, "No one is a good judge in his own case." The priest helps us arrive at an objective understanding of how we stand before God. There is great comfort in knowing we are truly forgiven — not just subjectively, but objectively.

In Confession, too, we may get some spiritual guidance. We may need counsel on how to deal with a problem in a truly Christian way. The priest can often help us find the right approach.

## Yearly Obligation

There is another reason to go to Confession. The *Catechism of the Catholic Church* states: "According to the Church's command, 'after having attained the age of discretion, each of the faithful is bound by an obligation faithfully to confess serious sins at least once a year'" (no. 1457). Each year we put off confessing serious sins, alas, another serious sin is added.

## Sacrament of Mercy

As anyone who has gone to Confession recently knows, the sacrament of Penance is not a harsh tribunal of justice but a manifestation of God's infinite mercy. God waits patiently for us to return to Him so that He can embrace us again with His love and help us to be at peace. The priest is there in the confessional to represent

---

[142] "[Jesus] breathed on them and said to them, "Receive the Holy Spirit. If you forgive the sins of any, they are forgiven them; if you retain the sins of any, they are retained" (John 20:22–23).

Christ, who told the parables of the lost sheep and the prodigal son, who forgave His executioners from the Cross. This is the Jesus who waits for you in the person of the priest in the confessional!

## Painful Sacrament?

In his autobiography, Fulton Sheen tells a story that shows this in action:

> I remember a stewardess on an international airline who began instructions [in Catholicism]. When we came to the subject of confession and sin, she said that she could not continue. I begged her to take one more hour of instruction, and then if she did not like what was said, she could leave.
>
> At the end of the second hour on that subject, she became almost violent and shouted: "Now I'll never join the Church after what I have heard about confessing sin." I said to her: "There is no proportion whatever between what you have heard and the way you are acting. Have you ever had an abortion?" She hung her head in shame and admitted that she had.
>
> That was the difficulty; it was not the sacrament of Penance. Later on I received her into the Church and baptized her first child.[143]

With that admission she found peace. She feared the pain of confessing but was extremely glad when it was over.

Sometimes, by avoiding a painful thing today we bring on twice the pain tomorrow. There is another thing to remember about the discomfort of this sacrament: the more we go, the easier

---

[143] Sheen, *Treasure in Clay*, 278–279.

it is to go. Everyone should attempt to go to Confession once a month. The more often we go to Confession, the more sensitive we are to our sins, even our small sins, and the less discomfort we feel in confessing them.

## Psychological Benefits

Many psychologists have marveled at the power of this sacrament. It is not primarily a psychological exercise, but there is a psychological benefit. We are told that strong emotions need to be expressed in some healthy way. If we keep them in, we may develop a neurosis. Guilt can be a strong and helpful emotion, if we allow it to move us to seek forgiveness. If we hold it in, however, it will pop out in other ways, as toothpaste used to come out of the side of the metal tube when we squeezed the tube without removing the cap. Guilt will come out as criticism, especially of the Church. Or it may come out as anger over any little thing that happens. Unexpressed guilt can make us very sour people.

Guilt leading to Confession and reform is quite different from a guilt trip. A guilt trip is being made to feel unwarranted or excessive guilt over something we have done. Not good. Guilt leading to Confession, reform, and making amends is good.

Dr. John Rathbone Oliver, an Episcopalian minister and a well-known psychiatrist, was praying in a Catholic church one Saturday afternoon while confessions were being heard. He said he saw a young girl in front of him, sixteen years old at most. She was quite tense, "tormented, apparently." She was in constant motion, turning one way and another. She appeared to be seriously upset.

> I could not take my eyes from her. She seemed anxiety personified. A few moments later, she got up, and went

into the confessional. I also got up, from my knees, and walked up to the high altar to kneel before the Blessed Sacrament. Time passed quickly there. Then someone pushed by me and knelt down on the altar steps, just a few feet away. It was the same girl. But I have never seen such a change in any human being.

All her tenseness was gone; the lines of worry had been smoothed from her face. No signs of mental torment now; no anxiety—only perfect relaxation, peace—and, apparently, a great happiness—for her lips were parted in a smile. If I, as a psychiatrist, could have done for that girl in three hours what had been accomplished in fifteen minutes, I should have thought myself a clever physician indeed.

I watched her make the sign of the cross, from forehead to breast, from shoulder to shoulder, with a hand that was steady, co-ordinated, efficient, exact. Then she folded her arms on her breast, and lifted her face to the Tabernacle. That face still bore traces of dried tears; but the eyes were bright, unclouded. I left her there, with a prayer of thanksgiving ... at peace with man—and if I may say so without irreverence, at home with her God.

"All magic, all superstition, all emotional self-hypnosis," my materialistic friends may say. Well, let them say so as often as they please. I shall begin to listen to them when their own particular type of magic and hypnosis gets the same results.[144]

[144] Rev. John A. O'Brien, *The Faith of Millions: The Credentials of the Catholic Religion* (Huntington, IN: Our Sunday Visitor, 1974), 188.

## Embarrassed to Confess to a Human Being

True, it can be embarrassing to confess to a human being, but that should not keep us from so great a source of grace. How often we confide in a friend the wrong we have done. Do we believe it is Jesus in the confessional, or not? Who could be a more understanding friend? I have received more understanding and comfort from the priests in the confessional than from any good friend.

What will the priest think of you? He will see you as Jesus sees you: one who has come to be wiped clean. "But won't he look down on me?" you wonder. Let the priest without sin be the first to throw a stone. We priests have to go to Confession too. Do you think we are without sin? Think again. Priests know also that some of the greatest saints—St. Augustine, St. Mary Magdalene, St. Margaret of Cortona—had been great sinners. Who is to say you are not the next sinner to become a saint? Priests try to look at the "new you," not the old one.

The priest is bound not only never to reveal the sins of a penitent but to try to forget sins as soon as he hears them. There is an expression that we priests have: What I know from Confession, I know less than that which I do not know at all.

## Conversion

So often Confession is the beginning of a great conversion. In one of his lectures, Archbishop Sheen told this story:

> When Charles de Foucauld, a hero of France but still an evil man, entered a church one day, he knocked at the confessional of Father Huvelin and said: "Come out, I want to talk to you about a problem." Fr. Huvelin answered, "No, come in; I want to talk to you about your sins." Foucauld,

struck by Divine Grace, obeyed; later on he became a [hermit] in the desert and one of the saintly men of our times.

Foucauld was beatified by Pope Benedict XVI in 2005, and his canonization has been approved by Pope Francis.

A friend once gave a talk to our women's group about his conversion. He had been a Catholic since childhood, but he fell into sin and neglected Confession, though he continued to go to Mass. So he did need conversion. He went to confess one Saturday afternoon and found himself at the end of a long line of people. He looked at his watch and decided he didn't have time to go, so he started to leave. A woman close to the confessional grabbed him as he went by and said, "Here, take my place. You look like you may need it more than I." Indeed he did. He was caught—by the Hound of Heaven. He went in, confessed, and returned to the sacraments for the first time in over ten years. He went on to become a very good priest.

## Just Venial Sins

St. John Paul II said:

> The Sacrament of Reconciliation is not reserved only for those who commit grave sins. It was instituted for the remission of all sins, and the grace that flows from it has a special efficacy of purification and support in the effort of amendment and progress. It is an irreplaceable sacrament in the Christian life; it cannot be despised or neglected if the seed of divine life is to develop in the Christian and give all the desired fruits.[145]

---

[145] Pope John Paul II, General Audience (June 15, 1983), Google translation of Italian original.

# Overcoming Sinful Thoughts

When we confess just venial sins, we develop a greater sensitivity to them and become more inclined to overcome them. Most people who commit mortal sins begin with repeated venial sins and, thus weakened, fall into more serious sins.

A man went to Confession during a retreat. It had been more than two years since he had gone. He hadn't committed any mortal sins, so he didn't absolutely have to go. Nonetheless, the priest gently corrected him on his staying away for so long. "Could it be a matter of pride that you haven't come to Confession all this time?" He encouraged him to go at least once a month from then on, just for venial sins. The man admitted his pride and resolved to go monthly.

Pius XII wrote in *Mystici Corporis*:

> For a constant and speedy advancement in the path of virtue we highly recommend the pious practice of frequent confession ... for by this means we grow in a true knowledge of ourselves and in Christian humility, bad habits are uprooted, spiritual negligence and apathy are prevented, the conscience is purified and the will strengthened, salutary spiritual direction is obtained and grace is increased by the effectiveness of the sacrament itself.[146]

Confession is the tribunal of God's fathomless mercy. God doesn't need it. We do.

---

[146] Pope Pius XII, Encyclical Letter *Mystici Corporis Christi* (On the Mystical Body of Christ) (June 29, 1943), no. 88.

26

# "I Don't Think There Is a Hell"

Over the last twenty years, the number of Americans who believe in the fiery down under has dropped from 71 percent to 58 percent. Heaven, by contrast, fares much better and, among Christians, remains an almost universally accepted concept.

Underlying these statistics is a conundrum that continues to tug at the consciences of some Christians, who find it difficult to reconcile the existence of a just, loving God with a doctrine that dooms countless people to eternal punishment. "Everlasting torment is intolerable from a moral point of view because it makes God into a bloodthirsty monster who maintains an everlasting Auschwitz for victims whom he does not even allow to die," wrote the late Clark Pinnock, an influential evangelical theologian.[147]

Some evangelical theologians, including Edward Fudge, are proposing what is called annihilationism, suggesting that, once a sinner dies, he is terminated, nonexistent. That would be more merciful than eternal suffering. That idea is not new. Some theologians proposed that in the second century.

---

[147] Quoted in Mark Strauss, "The Campaign to Eliminate Hell," *National Geographic*, May 13, 2016, https://www.nationalgeographic.com/news/2016/05/160513-theology-hell-history-christianity/.

In the third century, Origen held that one day hell would end, and all the souls there would enter heaven. That, of course, would not be hell but purgatory. However, the Church condemned this idea, declaring that the punishment of hell would last for all eternity (Fourth Lateran Council). This was no doubt based on the use of the word *eternal* or *everlasting* in Scripture when describing the punishment of hell (Matt. 25:41, 46; 2 Thess. 1:9).

St. Augustine wrote, "[Hell] is not a matter of feeling, but a fact.... There is no way of waiving or weakening the words which the Lord has told us He will pronounce at the Last Judgment."[148]

So what *did* Jesus say? "Enter through the narrow gate; for the gate is wide and the road is easy that leads to destruction, and there are many who take it. For the gate is narrow and the road is hard that leads to life, and there are few who find it" (Matt. 7:13–14).

And in the parable of the sheep and goats: "Then he will say to those at his left hand, 'You that are accursed, depart from me into the eternal fire prepared for the devil and his angels; for I was hungry and you gave me no food, I was thirsty and you gave me nothing to drink" (Matt. 25:41–42).

St. Teresa of Ávila relates the following:

> While I was at prayer one day, I suddenly found that, without knowing how, I had seemingly been put in Hell. I understood that the Lord wanted me to see the place the devils had prepared there for me and which I merited because of my sins....

---

[148] *City of God*, bk. 22, chap. 23, as quoted in John A. Hardon, SJ, "Demonology," The Real Presence Association, http://www.therealpresence.org/archives/Demonology/Demonology_002.htm.

I felt a fire in the soul that I don't know how I could describe. The bodily pains were so unbearable that, though I had suffered excruciating ones in this life, and according to what the doctors say, the worst that can be suffered on earth (for all my nerves were shrunken when I was paralyzed ...), these were nothing in comparison with what I experienced there. I saw furthermore that they would go on without end.... This, however, was nothing next to the soul's agonizing: a constriction, a suffocation, an affliction so keenly deeply felt ... that I don't know how to word it strongly enough.[149]

St. Maria Faustina relates a vision she had of hell:

Today, I was led by an angel to the chasm of Hell. It is a place of great torture; how awesomely large and extensive it is! ... I would have died at the very sight of these tortures if the omnipotence of God had not supported me. Let the sinner know that he will be tortured throughout all eternity, in those senses which he made use of to sin. I am writing this at the command of God, so that no soul may find an excuse by saying there is no Hell, or that nobody has ever been there, and so no one can say what it is like.[150]

Granted, the visions of the saints do not carry the same weight as Sacred Scripture and the teaching of Church councils.

[149] St. Teresa of Ávila *The Book of Her Life*, in *The Collected Works of St. Teresa of Ávila*, vol. 1, trans. Kieran Kavanaugh, OCD, and Otilio Rodriguez, OCD (Washington, DC: ICS Publications, 1976), 213.
[150] *Diary*, no. 741.

Nonetheless, their visions should be carefully considered, especially since they seem to be quite compatible with Scripture and Tradition.

Anglican theologian C. S. Lewis has a good answer to those who doubt the scriptural description of hell:

> In the long run, the answer to all those who object to the doctrine of Hell, is itself a question: "What are you asking God to do?" To wipe out their past sins, and at all costs, to give them a fresh start, smoothing over every difficulty and offering every miraculous help? But He has done so, on Calvary. To forgive them? They will not be forgiven. To leave them alone? Alas, I am afraid that is what He does.[151]

There is in the end only one type of person who will end in hell: the one who refuses God's mercy.

---

[151] C. S. Lewis, *The Problem of Pain* (New York: Macmillan, 1967), 130.

27

# "I Pray a Little Every Day and Attend Sunday Mass; That's Enough"

Does Sacred Scripture have any clues as to how much we should pray and pursue other spiritual exercises? It does. For starters,

> Just then a lawyer stood up to test Jesus. "Teacher," he said, "what must I do to inherit eternal life?" He said to him, "What is written in the law? What do you read there?" He answered, "You shall love the Lord your God with all your heart, and with all your soul, and with all your strength, and with all your mind; and your neighbor as yourself." And he said to him, "You have given the right answer; do this, and you will live." (Luke 10:25–28)[152]

To love someone with all one's heart, soul, strength, and mind is to make that person your first love. And loving someone calls for communication. It should be clear that communication with our first love should be strong.

Another Scripture passage that implies a strong devotion to God is from Leviticus: "You shall be holy, for I the Lord your

---

[152] This passage is the most important in the entire Bible.

God am holy" (Lev. 19:2; see also 1 Pet. 1:16). Has anyone ever become holy without prayer — a good amount of prayer?

It was often by example that Jesus taught us to pray. "And after he had dismissed the crowds, he went up the mountain by himself to pray. When evening came, he was there alone" (Matt. 14:23). And He prayed all night before choosing His apostles: "Now during those days he went out to the mountain to pray; and he spent the night in prayer to God. And when day came, he called his disciples and chose twelve of them, whom he also named apostles" (Luke 6:12–13). More examples of Jesus going off to pray include the following: "In the morning, while it was still very dark, he got up and went out to a deserted place, and there he prayed" (Mark 1:35); and "he would withdraw to deserted places and pray" (Luke 5:16).

## The Saints and Prayer

The saints spent long hours in prayer. When he was a student, his friends reported that John of the Cross studied very hard and spent hours each night in prayer. Later, as a superior in his order, he would often take his friars into the country and send each one out from the group to take up to two hours to communicate his appreciation to God for the gift of nature. They often had to go looking for John after the appointed time, only to find him completely engrossed in his prayer. When John was in Segovia, he would enter into contemplation for hours, or spend the night stretched out on the ground, taking in the sounds and beauty of nature.

When John Vianney was seven, he helped shepherd the family flock of sheep. Occasionally he would arrange for his shepherd friend to cover for him while he went and prayed, at times for hours. From the time he was a student, John would get up early (four o'clock) to pray before the Blessed Sacrament. When he was pastor at Ars, he got up even earlier to pray before the Blessed Sacrament because, as his biographer wrote, "the tabernacle attracted him irresistibly." Following their pastor's example, more and more parishioners spent long periods in adoration before the tabernacle. One such man, when asked what he did during his long visits in church, responded, "I just look at the good Lord, and he looks at me." Father Vianney told this story often, and added, "Everything is in that, my children."

St. Margaret Mary's brother Chrysostom said she prayed long into the night as a young girl. Sometimes the servants discovered that Margaret had prayed all night without sleeping, so absorbed was she in prayer. When she prayed before the Blessed Sacrament, she would not pray vocal prayers, such as the Our Father or the Hail Mary, but became so taken up with the meditative prayer Jesus taught her that she never tired. She wrote that she could pray before the tabernacle for hours, even days, without meals, conscious only of her Lord. When she entered a church, she would always go as close as possible to the tabernacle to have Jesus consume her in His love. When she was in the Visitation Order, whenever the other sisters couldn't find her, they knew where to look: in the chapel, praying before the tabernacle. She would spend long hours there, kneeling absolutely motionless, with her hands folded in prayer and her eyes shut tight. The sisters could not stir her by tapping her on the shoulder, but when they mentioned "obedience" she came immediately to her senses and went where they asked.

St. Margaret of Cortona, after turning from her nine-year sinful life as a mistress, attended Mass each day, spent long hours in prayer, worked as a midwife nurse helping to deliver babies, and cared for the poor. Every day, she would go early to the church to pray the Divine Office with the Franciscans and attend their Mass. Then she would meditate on the "book of love," namely, the crucifix, the book "written in every language … or, better, the language of the heart,… with the blood of Christ." In the evenings she would return to the church for prayer, sometimes continuing through the night. At another time, when parents brought their son, possessed by a demon, from another city to Margaret in Cortona, the evil spirit left him as they approached the town. The demon indicated that he could not stand the air filled with Margaret's prayers.

St. Monica pleaded endlessly to God for her son Augustine, while fasting, praying, and weeping in church long into the night. When Augustine snuck off to Rome at age twenty-nine without his mother, she prayed all night in the church near the dock from which he sailed, not realizing his trick.[153]

The child saint Dominic Savio loved to pray, and he prayed with such reverence, such devotion, that he inspired others, including adults. He would often go into the church with a friend to pray for the souls in purgatory. And he had a great devotion to the Blessed Virgin Mary. He would often kneel at her statue, saying, "Mother, I always want to be your son. Let me die rather than commit a single sin against [purity]." Every Friday he stopped in the church to pray, bringing classmates with him, to offer special prayers to Mary.

"Well, Father, those were saints. I'm not a saint."

What is a saint? Someone who was truly holy. But remember the words recorded in Sacred Scripture for all of us: "Be holy for I the Lord your God am holy." What is a saint if he or she is not someone who was holy? God has invited each one of us to be holy!

---

[153] Some months later, she caught up with him in Milan. After twelve years of her constant prayer, he was baptized at age thirty-two.

You need not be a canonized saint to have a strong prayer life. My own mother used to pray fifteen mysteries of the Rosary daily in addition to attending daily Mass. EWTN host Johnnette Benkovic mentioned on a telecast that her grandmother used to say thirteen Rosaries each day, one for each of her grandchildren. When I was in the seminary, one of my classmates mentioned that he had an uncle who prayed ten Rosaries a day.

Sacred Scripture encourages us to pray constantly: "Rejoice always, pray without ceasing, give thanks in all circumstances; for this is the will of God in Christ Jesus for you. Do not quench the Spirit" (1 Thess. 5:16–19). Not praying is a spiritual killer. St. Alphonsus Liguori wrote, "Those who pray are certainly saved; those who do not pray are certainly damned."[154]

## Prayer for Understanding

Praying a great deal does not guarantee our holiness, but it certainly helps. We still must make good choices about our lifestyles, but we need the grace that prayer brings to have the wisdom and strength to make these choices. In fact, we need prayer even to understand Scripture.

In my mid-twenties (long before I entered the seminary), I had a lapsed Catholic girlfriend who asked me to read a book titled *The Passover Plot*, which suggested that Jesus didn't really die on the Cross and just reappeared after a couple of days—a preposterous idea that presumed that the apostles were suckers. I wrote a short review of the book and gave it to her. Then I asked her to read my book. "What is your book?" she asked. "The

---

[154] Quoted in CCC 2744.

Gospel of Matthew," I answered. She agreed, so I lent her my new *Jerusalem Bible*, which I found to be delightful.

Some weeks later, she returned it and told me she had read it. I asked, "So, what did you think?" Her reply was an irreverent, "Eh." It was then that I realized that without prayer and humility, we cannot even understand Sacred Scripture. St. Augustine read the Bible before his conversion but didn't understand it. He wrote later about this: "I sought with pride what only humility could make me find ... and I fell to the ground."[155]

## Marriage with God

Why are we told to be holy as the heavenly Father is holy? Because we are called to a kind of marriage with God.

> As a young man marries a virgin
> your Builder shall marry you;
> And as a bridegroom rejoices in his bride
> so shall your God rejoice in you. (Isa. 62:5, NABRE)

St. Gregory the Great taught, "The husband of every Christian soul is God for she is joined to him by faith."[156] If we are to be in a marriage with someone who is holy, we need to be holy.

## Perfection and Holiness

As we've seen, Christ commanded us to be holy (Matt. 5:48). When we begin to pull together the sayings in Scripture about

---

[155] Quoted in Alban Butler, *Lives of the Saints*, selected and edited by Msgr. Goddard (London: R. Washbourne, 1883), 66.
[156] *The Sunday Sermons of the Great Fathers*, vol. 3, ed. M. F. Toal (San Francisco: Ignatius Press, 1996), 186.

what God expects, we should realize that He asks a great deal from us. Our prayer life, our sacramental life, our life of service to those in need should reflect the fact that we are striving to fulfill His request.

Unfortunately, as experience shows, we cannot create a strong prayer life overnight. We have to grow into a robust spiritual life, little by little, *poco a poco*. It's like the tiny mustard seed Jesus spoke of: "The kingdom of heaven is like a mustard seed that someone took and sowed in his field; it is the smallest of all the seeds, but when it has grown it is the greatest of shrubs and becomes a tree, so that the birds of the air come and make nests in its branches" (Matt. 13:31–32).

We begin small but keep growing until, like the full-grown mustard tree, we have a flourishing spirituality.

The best approach, it seems, is to commit to a small amount of prayer each day, perhaps five or ten minutes initially. St. Thérèse of Lisieux said, "It is better to take on only what you think you can persevere in."[157] How important to follow this way in the development of our prayer lives, to avoid growing too fast, lest we fall back to nothing.

In fact, some years back, I gave a talk to young adults in Washington, DC, and mentioned the importance of having a good, strong prayer life. One young man decided he would start a strong prayer life the next day. He began to pray the Rosary daily, attend daily Mass, make visits to the Blessed Sacrament, and read about the saints. He continued with this for two weeks. Then he fell back to almost nothing. He had set himself a challenge too great to sustain.

Pope St. Gregory the Great wrote, "When one wishes to reach the top of a mountain, he must climb by stages and step

---

[157] O'Mahony, *St. Thérèse of Lisieux*, 135.

by step, not by leaps and bounds."[158] And St. Philip Neri cautioned, "One should not wish to become a saint in four days but step by step."[159]

A person might make a commitment of five or ten minutes of prayer each day and then try to grow some every year. But how can you make God number one with just five minutes of prayer a day? By making that the most important five minutes of your day. Build your entire day around those five minutes, and try never to miss. And plan your entire weekend around Sunday Mass! We must make a commitment in order to do that. A prayer life that is hit or miss is not in any way making God first. That's like telling God, "If I have time, I will pray." Not good.

The first commitment to pray is the most difficult, and the first minute of prayer is the hardest. It is much harder to commit to five minutes of prayer each day after being used to no commitment, than to go from five to ten minutes or even fifteen minutes. St. John Vianney said just about as much when he preached: "The more you pray, the more you want to pray."[160] Unfortunately, the opposite is also true. The less you pray, the less you want to pray.

St. Teresa of Ávila was extremely bored by prayer. She felt so miserable when it was time to enter the chapel for meditative prayer, she had to force herself to go in to pray. She could hardly wait for the hour to be up. Nonetheless, after she made herself do this, she often felt better about her prayer time than

---

[158] "Letter to Abbot Mellitus," *Epistola* 76, *PL* 77: 1215–1216.

[159] Quoted in Alban Butler, *The Lives of the Fathers, Martyrs, and Other Principal Saints*, vol. 5 (Dublin: James Duffy, 1866; Bartleby.com, 2010), 147.

[160] Jill Haak Adels, *The Wisdom of the Saints* (New York: Oxford University Press, 1989), 40.

when she felt like praying![161] Later, Teresa wrote that when she abandoned prayer, it was no more than "putting myself right in Hell without the need of devils,"[162] and "There is but one road which reaches God and that is prayer; if anyone shows you another, you are being deceived."[163] This transformation of Teresa is typical of many who begin to pray. It is extremely difficult at first to get into the habit, but once people have gotten through that difficulty, they begin to love prayer, especially when they see what it does for them.

How much would be enough as a final goal to fulfill the command of Jesus, to love God with all our heart, soul, mind, and strength—let's say, by the time we are sixty or seventy, assuming that we begin to grow in our twenties or thirties? Perhaps 10 percent of our waking hours. That would be a tithe. God asks a tithe of our income in Sacred Scripture. Perhaps a tithe of our time would be acceptable.

For some, that might seem daunting, but again, the more you pray, the more you want to pray. I began to pray the Rosary daily (in bed, at night) when I was a freshman in high school. By my junior year, I noticed how my life had changed for the better. "I'm never going to stop this. It's working," were my thoughts. That often happens when we develop a decent prayer life. We begin to see the effects, and we realize we don't ever want to stop.

I never dreamed at age twenty-five that I would pray as much as I do now. And I'll bet most of the saints, when they were

---

[161] *The Autobiography of St. Teresa of Ávila*, trans. Kieran Kavanaugh, OCD, and Otilio Rodriguez, OCD (New York: Book-of-the-Month Club, 1995), chap. 8, para. 7, p. 68.

[162] *Autobiography*, chap. 19, para. 4, p. 124.

[163] Quoted in Fr. Daniel Haggerty, *The Contemplative Hunger* (San Francisco: Ignatius Press, 2016), 21.

younger, did not anticipate they would ever pray as much as they prayed. So we need not think of our goal starting out. We should just ask God to lead us to the prayer life He wants us to have.

## Consequences of a Modest Prayer Life

"Are you telling me that if I don't have a strong prayer life, I am displeasing God?" Not exactly. If you are not trying to be holy, you are displeasing God. If you are not trying to love God with all your heart, soul, and mind, you are displeasing God. If you are not trying to be perfect as your heavenly Father is perfect, you are displeasing God. And it seems logical that all those things call for a strong life of prayer (and more). Granted, it may take some time to ramp up to that level of prayer, but that should be the primary item on your to-do list.

There is another consequence of having only a modest prayer life: it will make it difficult for us to understand Sacred Scripture and the moral teachings of the Church. The grace that comes from prayer opens our hearts to understand God's Word and gives us the strength to live it. This grace helps us to be open to what we read in the lives of the saints; it opens us to be willing to pursue an even richer spiritual life and to attend Mass more frequently than just on Sundays. The words of Jesus apply: "Pay attention to what you hear; the measure you give will be the measure you get, and still more will be given you. For to those who have, more will be given; and from those who have nothing, even what they have will be taken away" (Mark 4:24–25).

A further consequence of having a modest prayer life is that you might cause yourself to be a candidate for purgatory. As we will see in the next chapter, purgatory is no picnic. In fact, it is *extremely* painful.

## Daily Mass?

The greatest spiritual activity we could ever participate in is the Mass. The Mass, the Eucharistic Sacrifice is, as the Second Vatican Council taught, "the source and summit of the Christian life."[164] Why? Because it is the re-offering of the one sacrifice of Jesus on the Cross, the event that saved us. The *Catechism of the Catholic Church* teaches: "In this divine sacrifice which is celebrated in the Mass, the same Christ who offered himself once in a bloody manner on the altar of the cross is contained and is offered in an unbloody manner" (1367). What could be more powerful?

The saints spoke eloquently about the glory of the Mass:

If we really understood the Mass, we would die of joy.... All good works taken together cannot have the value of one Holy Mass, because they are the works of men, whereas the Holy Mass is the work of God. (St. John Vianney)[165]

One single Mass gives more honor to God than ... all the prayers and penances of the saints, the labors of the apostles, all the torments of the martyrs and all the burning love of the seraphim and of the divine Mother. (St. Alphonsus Liguori)[166]

If the Mass is so powerful—the greatest source of holiness—and we must be so holy to be worthy of the kingdom, should we not consider the possibility of attending daily Mass? I prayed for

[164] Second Vatican Council, *Lumen Gentium*, no. 11.
[165] Quoted in Stefano Manelli, FFI, *Jesus, Our Eucharistic Love* (New Bedford, MA: Academy of the Immaculate, 1996), 30.
[166] St. Alphonsus Liguori, *The Holy Mass* (New York: Benziger Bros., 1889), 310.

years implicitly that I might one day participate in Mass every day. At age thirty-two, two years before entering the seminary, I committed to start. It was not without concern that getting up early enough for seven o'clock Mass might cause me health problems. I resolved to continue for three months and, if it didn't kill me, I would continue for life. Not only did it not kill me, but after three weeks, my health actually *improved*. I have continued to this day. What a grace from God!

A lawyer friend told me he wanted to ease into daily Mass. So, the first year he went one extra day besides Sunday, the second year two days, and so on. After six years he was going every day. Wonderful!

When people come to me for spiritual direction, I often ask if they are attending Mass daily. If they say no, I ask if they would be willing to pray, "Lord, if you would like me to go to Mass daily, please arrange it." When they do, more often than not, within a year their job or their residence changes so they *can* attend. It seems this is the type of prayer that God wants to answer!

## How to Stay Motivated

We all know that as time goes on, we tend to slack off in our spiritual activities. How do we stay "up" for prayer and our other spiritual exercises? By reading: reading Sacred Scripture and the lives and writings of the saints. I recommend reading the Mass readings for the next day and five to ten pages daily in the lives or writings of the saints — never more than ten pages daily of the latter. Spiritual reading is not like recreational reading. That is done for enjoyment. Spiritual reading is for formation.

St. Athanasius of Alexandria wrote, "You will not see anyone who is truly striving after his spiritual advancement who is not given to spiritual reading,"[167] and St. Padre Pio taught, "The harm that comes to souls from the lack of reading holy books makes me shudder.... What power spiritual reading has to lead to a change of course, and to make even worldly people enter into the way of perfection."[168]

## Prayer versus Work

One young adult asked me, "So how do you decide between prayer or weekday Mass or other spiritual activities and work? How do you make the trade-off?" My answer is that as you grow in prayer and you see how it is making a difference, you should gradually move toward a stronger spiritual life as a priority over some work options.

For example, a young man in one of my parishes used to work seven days a week in his construction business. One day, a light went on and he realized he should, as a Christian, refrain from working on Sundays. He thought that once he got into his new schedule, his income would go down and he was willing to accept that. It didn't. In fact, it went up!

When I was in the seminary, as I increased my prayer, I discovered I was able to study faster. I lost nothing by increasing my prayer time.

So, as we continue to grow, prayer and other spiritual activities become greater and greater priorities. It's analogous to finding

---

[167] Quoted in Ronda Chervin, *Quotable Saints* (Ann Arbor, MI: Servant Books, 1992), 138.

[168] See my recommended spiritual reading list at https://cfalive.com/pages/a-guide-to-spiritual-reading-for-adults. To download free books on the saints, go to Free Traditional Catholic Books, http://www.traditionalcatholic.co/free-catholicbooks/.

a new girlfriend. You make time for her because she becomes a priority. It just comes naturally.

## Well, I'm a Good Person

Sometimes we hear, "I'm a good person. I don't hurt people. I will be saved." I have heard that often, but I have researched the Scriptures for forty years and have never seen the words "Be a good person and don't hurt anyone, and you will be saved." Sacred Scripture says rather, "Be holy," and "Be perfect."

"Well, I keep the commandments. Why wouldn't I be saved?" What about the greatest commandment, "Love God with all your heart," and, the second, "Love your neighbor as yourself"? Loving your neighbor means more than doing him or her no harm. It means actively trying to make your neighbor's life better.

Holy people are not just concerned about keeping the Ten Commandments (although that is certainly part of it). They are trying to live out the virtues: the theological virtues of faith, hope and love; and the cardinal virtues of prudence, justice, temperance, and fortitude. In other words, to be holy is not just to avoid evil but to form habits of doing good.[169]

## I Love God in My Own Way

When a young boy gives his mother a football for her birthday, she may smile and graciously accept it. If he does the same when

[169] The best books I have seen on the virtues are *Faith, Hope, Love* (Ignatius Press, 1997) and *The Four Cardinal Virtues: Prudence, Justice, Fortitude, Temperance* (University of Notre Dame Press, 1965), both by Josef Pieper.

he is thirty-five, there is something terribly wrong in his understanding of love.

It is the same when a Christian loves God "in his own way." If we are going to love someone, we must love that person in the way he or she wants to be loved. And Jesus has told us how to love Him: "Very truly, I tell you, unless you eat the flesh of the Son of Man and drink his blood, you have no life in you. Those who eat my flesh and drink my blood have eternal life, and I will raise them up on the last day" (John 6:53–54).

Jesus provides another condition for salvation: "Very truly, I tell you, no one can enter the kingdom of God without being born of water and Spirit. What is born of the flesh is flesh, and what is born of the Spirit is spirit. Do not be astonished that I said to you, 'You must be born from above'" (John 3:5–7).

He also said:

> "Not everyone who says to me, "Lord, Lord," will enter the kingdom of heaven, but only the one who does the will of my Father in heaven. On that day many will say to me, "Lord, Lord, did we not prophesy in your name, and cast out demons in your name, and do many deeds of power in your name?" Then I will declare to them, "I never knew you; go away from me, you evildoers." (Matt. 7:21–23)

St. Paul spells out the things that would keep us from making it to the kingdom: "Do you not know that wrongdoers will not inherit the kingdom of God? Do not be deceived! Fornicators, idolaters, adulterers, male prostitutes, sodomites, thieves, the greedy, drunkards, revilers, robbers—none of these will inherit the kingdom of God" (1 Cor. 6:9–10).

Jesus and St. Paul laid down some essential conditions for salvation. If we want to be saved, we should heed those conditions and approach God in *His* way, not in ours.

∞

If God wants you to be holy as He says, a few prayers daily and Sunday Mass is not even close to being enough. Although we need not start with large amounts of prayer, we should grow in prayer slowly, steadily, until we spend a good deal of time with God each day, and that time should be our first priority. St. John Chrysostom captures the essence of this whole chapter:

> Prayer and converse with God is a supreme good: it is a partnership and union with God. As the eyes of the body are enlightened when they see light, so our spirit, when it is intent on God, is illumined by his infinite light. I do not mean the prayer of outward observance but prayer from the heart, not confined to fixed times or periods but continuous throughout the day and night.... Throughout the whole of our lives we may enjoy the benefit that comes from prayer if we devote a great deal of time to it.[170]

---

[170] Quoted in *Liturgy of the Hours*, Matins, Friday after Ash Wednesday.

28

# "I'm Just Aiming for Purgatory"

A person having a modest spiritual life but making every effort to live in the state of grace would be a candidate for purgatory. Dying in the state of grace ensures that a person is saved, even if the person needs to spend time in purgatory. What's wrong with that?

First of all, having a modest spiritual life may not be enough to stay in the state of grace, especially in this age. We are surrounded by so many evils—on television, in politics, on the Internet, and on social media—that we need all the grace we can get to avoid falling into these evils. A strong spiritual life is our plexiglass protection against all the temptations we face. In fact, we need a good deal of grace just to *see* the evil around us. Without strong grace, we will be caught up in condoning sin and living in it, without even recognizing that.

Think, for example, of the politician who wouldn't dream of missing Sunday Mass but supports legal abortion (for all nine months, in some cases!) and same-sex marriage. And he or she seems quite confident of being a "good Catholic" living in the state of grace. One might want to claim invincible or blameless ignorance, but ignorance on these issues is almost impossible for a civil or religious leader. The Church has been very clear on these things, and a whole lot of information is readily available on the Internet and in Catholic publications on these matters. A politician needs to know these moral issues.

## The Greatest Commandment

The second problem with this attitude is that it is a violation of what Jesus said was the first and greatest commandment.

> "Teacher, which commandment in the law is the greatest?" He said to him, "'You shall love the Lord your God with all your heart, and with all your soul, and with all your mind.' This is the greatest and first commandment. And a second is like it: 'You shall love your neighbor as yourself.' On these two commandments hang all the law and the prophets." (Matt. 22:36–40)

Those are commandments, not suggestions.

One need not be a rocket scientist—or a theologian—to realize that a modest spiritual life, such as a few prayers daily and Sunday Mass, would hardly be loving God with all your heart, soul, and mind for the average twenty-first-century Catholic.

Some may want to say, "Well that commandment is hyperbole." Is it? It matches pretty well with some other biblical teachings, some of which we saw in previous chapters, such as, "Be perfect, therefore, as your heavenly Father is perfect" (Matt. 5:48); "You shall be holy, for I the Lord your God am holy" (Lev. 19:2); "He chose us in Christ before the foundation of the world to be holy and blameless before him in love" (Eph. 1:4); and "May the God of peace himself sanctify you entirely; and may your spirit and soul and body be kept sound and blameless at the coming of our Lord Jesus Christ" (1 Thess. 5:23).

Vatican II speaks of this call to holiness: "Thus it is evident to everyone, that all the faithful of Christ of whatever rank or status, are called to the fullness of the Christian life and to the perfection of charity; by this holiness as such a more human manner of living is promoted in this earthly society."[171]

It seems that God really wants us to be holy. And he didn't say "You *should* be perfect" but "You *must* be perfect."

There are a number of quotes from the saints that support this theme. St. Dominic Savio, when asked what he wanted to do in life, answered, "I want to become a saint, and I will not be happy till I become one!"[172] St. Thérèse of Lisieux wrote, "You cannot be half a saint, you must be a whole saint or no saint at all."[173] And the spirit of St. Augustine is captured in this passage: "To fall in love with God is the greatest romance; to seek him the greatest adventure; to find him, the greatest human achievement."[174]

It's not only the saints who encouraged holiness. Devout French novelist Leon Bloy wrote, "The only real sadness, the only real failure, the only great tragedy in life, is not to become a saint."[175] St. Francis de Sales insisted that this call to holiness

---

[171] Second Vatican Council, *Lumen Gentium*, no. 40.
[172] From the *Life of Saint Dominic Savio* by St. John Bosco.
[173] Letter to Abbe Belliere, June 21, 1897, "Two Letters of St. Thérèse of Lisieux to Abbe Belliere," Ave Maria Press, https://www.avemariapress.com/engagingfaith/two-letters-st-therese-lisieux-abbe-belliere.
[174] This quotation has been attributed to St. Augustine, probably incorrectly. See "St. Augustine, Romance, Achievement, Adventure," Fauxtations, August 28, 2015, https://fauxtations.wordpress.com/2015/08/28/st-augustine-romance-adventure-achievement/.
[175] Quoted in Fr. John Riccardo, *Heaven Starts Now: Becoming a Saint Day by Day* (The Word Among Us, 2016).

applies to everyone: "All of us can attain to Christian virtue and holiness, no matter in what condition of life we live and no matter what our life work may be."[176] Pope Francis affirmed the same point: "To be saints is not a privilege for the few, but a vocation for everyone."[177]

So holiness is not merely the ideal for a Christian; it's the norm. Why? Because we are called to a kind of marriage with God, who by His nature cannot accept the smallest imperfection. In fact, He said as much to St. Margaret Mary, "Learn that I am a Holy Master and One that teaches holiness. I am pure and cannot endure the slightest stain."[178]

So, where would we go if we die in the state of grace and love God with most of our heart, soul, and mind, but not with *all* our heart, soul, and mind? We would go to purgatory.

## Do You Really Want to Go to Purgatory?

The purpose of purgatory is to make up for our sins that have been forgiven. Why do we need to do that? Didn't Jesus pay the price? Jesus paid a huge price for our sins—but not the whole price. St. Paul gave evidence of that when he wrote, "I am now rejoicing in my sufferings for your sake, and in my flesh I am completing what is lacking in Christ's afflictions for the sake of his body, that is, the church" (Col. 1:24).

The writings of St. Paul also furnish scriptural evidence for purgatory:

[176] Quoted in "St. Francis de Sales," https://catholicsaints.info/saint-francis-de-sales/.

[177] Pope Francis (@pontifex), Twitter, November 21, 2003.

[178] *The Autobiography of St. Margaret Mary* (Rockford, IL: TAN Books, 1986), 64.

Each one's work will become manifest; for the Day will disclose it, because it will be revealed with fire, and the fire will test what sort of work each one has done. If the work which any man has built on the foundation survives, he will receive a reward. If anyone's work is burned up, he will suffer loss, though he himself will be saved, but only as through fire. (1 Cor. 3:13–15)[179]

This purgation is necessary if we are to be united with God. St. Catherine of Genoa explained that "the divine essence is so pure and light-filled—much more than we can imagine—that the soul that has but the slightest imperfection would rather throw itself into a thousand hells than appear thus before the divine presence."[180]

Do we really think that if we fall far short of this perfection but die in the state of grace, Jesus will meet us at the gates of heaven and say, "That teaching on perfection (Matt. 5:48)—I didn't really mean it. Come on in"?

---

[179] Some other biblical passages that support the teaching on purgatory: "And in anger his lord handed him over to be tortured until he would pay his entire debt. So my heavenly Father will also do to every one of you, if you do not forgive your brother or sister from your heart" (Matt. 18:34–35). The implication here is that one may make up for sins after death. Also, in Maccabees we read, "Thus, he [Judas Maccabeus] made atonement for the dead that they might be absolved from their sin" (2 Macc. 12:46, NABRE). Prayer for the dead is linked to the doctrine of purgatory, since if the dead are in heaven or hell, there is no need or no reason to pray for them. See also Matthew 12:32.

[180] St. Catherine of Genoa, *Catherine of Genoa: Purgation and Purgatory* (Mahwah, NJ: Paulist Press, 1979), 78.

## The Pain and Joy of Purgatory

Purgatory will not be pleasant. St. Augustine taught, "This fire of Purgatory will be more severe than any pain that can be felt, seen or conceived in this world." As we saw earlier, Thomas Aquinas said something similar, that "the least pain of Purgatory surpasses the greatest pain of this life."[181]

At the same time, there is a positive side to purgatory. St. Francis de Sales, while admitting the harshness of purgatory, points out the joy there as well. The suffering souls' "bitterest anguish is soothed by a certain profound peace. It is a species of Hell as regards the suffering; it is a Paradise as regards the delight infused into their hearts by charity—a charity stronger than death and more powerful than Hell."[182]

Why is there such joy in purgatory? Because once there, we are assured of entering heaven one day. It's guaranteed.

Nevertheless, despite the joy of those being purified, the Church herself calls them the "Church Suffering," and I do not know of one holy soul in purgatory who has appeared to a saint—and a good number have appeared—and told them, "It's delightful here. Come and join me!" All have asked for prayers or penances or especially Masses to hasten their release.

## The Duration of Purgatory

St. Robert Bellarmine, Doctor of the Church, taught, "There is no doubt that the pains of Purgatory are not limited to

---

[181] Both quotations can be found in *Summa Theologiae*, appendix 1, q. 2, art. 1.

[182] St. Francis de Sales, in *Esprit de Francis de Sales*, chap. 9, p. 16, as quoted in Fr. F. X. Schouppe, *Purgatory Explained by the Lives and Legends of the Saints* (Rockford, IL: TAN Books, 1986), 26.

ten or twenty years, and that they last in some cases entire centuries."[183] And it seems that to the souls in purgatory the time seems much longer than the equivalent time on earth. St. Catherine of Genoa wrote, "If we regarded our own proper good, it would seem better to us to suffer here for a little than to remain in torments forever; better to suffer for a thousand years every woe possible to this body in this world, than to remain one hour in Purgatory."[184]

We speak of time in purgatory only analogously. Father Réginald Garrigou-Lagrange, a highly respected twentieth-century theologian, wrote:

Theological opinion, in general, favors long duration of purgatorial purification. Private revelations mention three or four centuries, or even more, especially for those who have had high office and great responsibility....

Purgatory is not measured by solar time, but by eviternity and discontinuous time. Discontinuous time ... is composed of successive spiritual instants, and each of these instants may correspond to ten, twenty, thirty, sixty hours of our solar time.[185]

(Eviternity, according to St. Thomas Aquinas, "differs from time, and from eternity, as the mean between them both."[186])

[183] Robert Bellarmine, *De Genitu*, bk. 2, chap. 9, as quoted in Schouppe, *Purgatory*, 68.
[184] *Life and Doctrine*, chap. 16.
[185] Réginald Garrigou-Lagrange, *Life Everlasting and the Immensity of the Soul: A Theological Treatise on the Four Last Things: Death, Judgment, Heaven, Hell* (Rockford, IL: TAN Books, 1991), 176–177.
[186] *Summa Theologiae*, I, q. 10, art. 5.

## How to Avoid Purgatory

One of the greatest ways to avoid purgatory is to attend Mass and receive Holy Communion daily. St. Peter Julian Eymard wrote, "The Mass is the most holy act of religion; you can do nothing that can give greater glory to God or be more profitable for your soul than to hear Mass both frequently and devoutly. It is the favorite devotion of the saints."[187] And St. Alphonsus Ligouri asserted, "Even God Himself could do nothing holier, better, nor greater than the Mass."[188]

There is another way to avoid purgatory: to receive indulgences. Of course, in the time of Martin Luther, there were abuses regarding indulgences, about which Luther rightly protested. At one point, a Dominican priest, Johann Tetzel proclaimed, "As soon as the coin in the coffer rings, the rescued soul to heaven springs." The Church strongly condemned such abuses.

Nonetheless, indulgences are still very much part of the teaching of the Church. The Council of Trent "condemns with anathema those who say that indulgences are useless or that the Church does not have the power to grant them."

The great benefit to be found in indulgences is brought out in the following account. St. Teresa of Ávila wrote of a religious sister who exercised great effort to gain every possible indulgence offered by the Church. Otherwise, she seemed to have an ordinary

---

[187] Quoted at Integrated Catholic Life, August 2, 2013, https://www.integratedcatholiclife.org/2013/08/daily-quote-from-st-peter-julian-eymard-2/.

[188] Quoted in Fr. Paul O'Sullivan, OP, "Daily Mass a Key to Heaven," from *The Wonders of the Mass*, excerpt posted at Catholic News World, January 24, 2016, http://www.catholic-newsworld.com/2016/01/daily-mass-key-to-heaven-quotes-to.html.

life and she was not particularly virtuous. She died, and Teresa was surprised to see her soul enter heaven almost right after her death. When Teresa expressed her surprise at this, our Lord told her, "It was by that means [the indulgences] that she had made up almost the whole of her debt, which was quite considerable, before her death; and therefore appeared with great purity before the tribunal of God."[189]

I give some details in the appendix on how to attain indulgences.

Granted, it is better to enter purgatory than to end up in hell. But purgatory is nothing to look forward to. It is a place or state of arduous suffering that souls must endure for not taking to heart the need to become holy, the need to become perfect as our heavenly Father is perfect, the need to become saints. God doesn't want us to go to purgatory. He would like us to avoid it and enter heaven immediately upon our death. Some saints have done just that. God wants us to do likewise.

---

[189] Schouppe, *Purgatory*, 255–256. It may sound as if this sister fell short of her Christian call to holiness, but we should remember that she *was* a religious sister, probably attending Mass daily and praying a good deal. We might guess she was pursuing holiness but was still short of her goal. Also, her indulgences brought her the merits of Mary and all the saints.

29

# "Heaven Sounds Boring to Me"

This idea that heaven might be boring is one of the reasons our young people — and some older people as well — drift away from the Faith, yet nothing could be further from the truth. As St. Paul wrote of heaven, "What no eye has seen, nor ear heard, nor the human heart conceived, what God has prepared for those who love him" (1 Cor. 2:9). It is beyond anything we can imagine.

But that is still a bit abstract for some, especially the young. More concretely, the saints have assured us that whatever enjoyment we experience here pales in comparison to what awaits us. St. Augustine wrote, "What, then, must be the consolations of the blessed, seeing that men on earth enjoy so much of so many and of such marvelous blessings?"[190] Teresa of Àvila remarked, "Our life lasts only a couple of hours. Our reward is boundless."[191] "I have formed such a high idea of heaven that, at times, I wonder what God will do at my death to surprise me," said St. Thérèse of Lisieux. "My hope is so great, it is such a subject of joy to me,

---

[190] *City of God*, bk. 22, chap. 24.
[191] *The Way of Perfection*, trans. E. Allison Peers (New York: Image Books, 1964), 43.

not by feeling but by faith, that to satisfy me fully something will be necessary which is beyond all human conception."[192]

If we knew a tiny fraction of the joy of heaven, we would work with a frenzy every day to make sure we get there. St. John of the Cross said the same thing more eloquently:

Were (the soul) to have but a foreglimpse of the height and beauty of God, she would not only desire death in order to see him now forever, as she here desires, but she would very gladly undergo a thousand singularly bitter deaths to see Him only for a moment; and having seen Him, she would ask to suffer just as many more that she might see Him for another moment.[193]

St. Gregory the Great said heaven would be like a marriage: "The husband of every Christian soul is God; for she is joined to Him by faith."[194] John of the Cross wrote along the same lines:

One does not reach this garden of full transformation which is the joy, delight and glory of spiritual marriage, without first passing through the spiritual espousal and the loyal and mutual love of betrothed persons. For, after the soul has been for some time the betrothed of the Son of God in gentle and complete love, God calls her and places her in His flowering garden to consummate this most joyful state of marriage with Him.... Yet in this life this union cannot be perfect, although it is beyond words and thought.[195]

[192] Sister of Jesus Agnes, *The Last Conversations of Saint Thérèse* (Long Prairie, MN: Neumann Press, 1998), 29.
[193] *Spiritual Canticle*, stanza 11.
[194] *Sunday Sermons*, vol. 3, 186.
[195] *Spiritual Canticle*, stanza 22.

Sts. Margaret of Cortona, Catherine of Siena, Lawrence Justinian, John of God, and John Vianney all received wedding rings from the Lord.[196] When St. Margaret Mary Alacoque suffered great temptations against her vocation to be a nun, Jesus appeared to her one day after Communion and showed her that He was "the most beautiful, the wealthiest, the most powerful, the most perfect and the most accomplished among all lovers."[197] He told her he had chosen her to be His spouse. Seeing that, she hesitated no longer.

There are several biblical passages that support this marriage-with-God theme. In Ezekiel 16, the Lord addresses His people, Jerusalem, as His unfaithful spouse with whom He later restores His covenant. In Isaiah we read:

> No more shall you be called "Forsaken,"
>     nor your land called "Desolate,"
> But you shall be called "My Delight is in her,"
>     and your land "Espoused."
> For the Lord delights in you,
>     and your land shall be espoused.
> For as a young man marries a virgin,
>     your Builder shall marry you;
> And as a bridegroom rejoices in his bride
>     so shall your God rejoice in you. (Isa. 62:4–5, NABRE)

Hosea 1 and 2 contain the story of God's relationship with Israel. First there is God's complaint: "The land commits great

---

[196] Abbé Francis Trochu, *The Curé d'Ars: St. Jean-Marie Baptiste Vianney*, trans. Dom Ernest Graf (Rockford, IL: TAN Books, 1977), 545.

[197] *Autobiography*, 40.

harlotry by forsaking the LORD" (1:2, RSVCE). Then God leads her back to Him and says after her return, "And I will betroth you to me forever; I will betroth you to me in righteousness and in justice, in steadfast love, and in mercy. I will betroth you to me in faithfulness; and you shall know the LORD" (2:19–20, RSVCE).[198]

Imagine, as I often do, the most beautiful person of the opposite sex you have ever seen, who happens to be God, coming to you, embracing you warmly, chastely, and whispering in your ear, "We will be married ... forever."[199] That is a bit more concrete.

Another thought about heaven: there is no time there. That does not mean that nothing is happening; it means, rather, that everything is happening there, all at once! Have you ever hugged someone and wished that hug could last forever? In heaven it can, and you can do a hundred other things at once. Nothing gets old in heaven, you never have to clean anything in heaven,

---

[198] Most of the above is adapted from my book, *Be Holy: A Catholic's Guide to the Spiritual Life* (Cincinnati: Servant Books, 2009), 5–10.

[199] This takes more imagination for men than for women, to be sure. However, the *Catechism of the Catholic Church* teaches, "We ought therefore to recall that God transcends the human distinction between the sexes. He is neither man nor woman: he is God" (239). We call Him by masculine names and pronouns because He has a male role in relationship to us (provider, pursuer, and so forth). Thus, the soul is always feminine in spiritual writing. Men who have difficulty imagining this embrace should realize that both men and women are created in the image and likeness of God. When a man sees the beauty of a woman, body and soul, he sees a reflection of the beauty of God.

It should be kept in mind that you should avoid using the image of a person whom you see often, lest you latch on to that person instead of God.

you never run out of supplies in heaven, and you need not wait for anything in heaven. You can move from place to place in "no time," and the weather is absolutely amazing.

Archbishop Sheen waxed eloquent about heaven:

> Time is the one thing that makes real pleasure impossible for the simple reason that it does not permit us to make a club sandwich of pleasures. By its nature it forbids us to have many pleasures together.... I know there are advertisements which invite us to dine and dance, but no one can do both comfortably at one and the same time. All things are good, and yet none can be enjoyed except in their season, and the enjoyment must always be tinged with the regret that time will demand their surrender. Time gives me things but it also takes them away.
>
> This thought suggests ... that if time makes the combination of pleasures impossible, then if I could ever transcend time, I might, in some way, increase my happiness, and this I find to be true, for every conscious desire to prolong a pleasure is the desire to make it an enduring "now." [200]

Of course, among the pleasures we will experience is the delight of warm, intimate friendships, not only with the God whose beauty and charm far surpass the most beautiful and charming persons on earth but also with the most fascinating, beautiful,[201] and gracious persons ever to have walked the face of the earth.

[200] Fulton J. Sheen, *Go to Heaven* (New York: McGraw-Hill, 1960), 226–228.
[201] In the kingdom we will be as beautiful as we were holy in this life.

# Overcoming Sinful Thoughts

We ought never allow a day to go by without thinking about the unfathomable joys of heaven, lest we forget our ultimate destination and why we are here on earth. And may we never fail to embrace in our hearts and minds every image of the final embrace with God and all His holy ones, and all His manifold pleasures in the eternal now of His kingdom.

30

# Common Threads

The many sinful thoughts identified in this book have some common threads. The first and most glaring thread is that they are anti-biblical. Pride is so clearly condemned in the Bible that one would have to be totally ignorant of Scripture to think that pride could be acceptable to God or to anyone else.

Most of these sinful thoughts are a product of being too focused on this world; of wanting recognition (pride), freedom from suffering (including loneliness), success here, good things (entitlement), answers to prayers, pleasure, or control; of avoiding embarrassment (same sins, leaving support group); of succumbing to worldly license or worldly comfort (including needing a sinful break and avoiding the cross).

Others involve going directly against Gospel teaching, including refusing to love enemies, refusing to help the poor, failing to pursue justice, settling for mediocrity, forming a weak view of the kingdom, and taking a self-centered and self-defeating approach to sin and the love of God.

The most fundamental moral conversion of a Christian is to embrace totally the truth that nothing in this world can satisfy our longing for happiness—nothing but God and the Life to which He calls us.

Appendix

# Indulgences[202]

An indulgence is a remission before God of the temporal punishment due to sins whose guilt has already been forgiven, which the faithful Christian who is duly disposed gains under certain prescribed conditions through the action of the Church which, as the minister of redemption, dispenses and applies with authority the treasury of the satisfactions of Christ and the saints. (CCC 1471)

Every sin, even venial, entails an unhealthy attachment to creatures, which must be purified either here on earth, or after death in the state called Purgatory. (CCC 1472)

To receive an indulgence, a person must have the (general, at least) intention to receive it. Indulgences may be offered for the dead or for the person performing the indulgenced work but not for another living person. There are two types of indulgences: plenary and partial.

---

[202] Excerpted from the author's article, "Helping the Souls in Purgatory," *Homiletic and Pastoral Review*, November 27, 2017, https://www.hprweb.com/2017/11/helping-the-souls-in-purgatory/.

## Plenary Indulgences

A plenary indulgence removes all temporal punishment due to sin. In other words, it eliminates entirely the need for purgatory at the time it is gained.

A plenary indulgence removes all *our* temporal punishment due to sin if offered for ourselves, but it does not necessarily do so for the dead person for whom we might offer it. For the dead, indulgences are offered by "suffrage," that is, as a prayer, without certainty that it is plenary. The effects of such an indulgence are "according to the hidden designs of God's mercy."[203] Nonetheless, such an indulgence would be a powerful aid to a person in purgatory.

To receive a plenary indulgence, the activity must be accompanied by the four requirements given below, in addition to the person's being in the state of grace. Only one plenary indulgence may be gained per day, except in danger of death.

*Four Conditions for Gaining a Plenary Indulgence*[204]

1.  Sacramental Confession within twenty days before or after the work
2.  Eucharistic Communion
3.  Prayer for the intention of the Holy Father (one Our Father and one Hail Mary suffice). It is "fitting" that receiving Communion and prayers for the Holy Father take place on the same day as the indulgenced work.
4.  Freedom from all attachment to sin, including venial sin. This does not mean *freedom from all sin*, but a sincere willingness to overcome every sin in your life.

---

[203] Bl. James Alberione, *Lest We Forget* (Boston: St. Paul Editions, 1967), 151.
[204] *Enchiridion of Indulgences*, "Norms on Indulgences," no. 26.

As we can see from this, attaining a plenary indulgence requires a commitment to strive for Christian perfection.

### Some Ways to Gain Plenary Indulgences

A plenary indulgence may be received for any of the following works on any day of the year (with the four requirements listed above):

1. Visit the Most Blessed Sacrament for at least one half hour.
2. Recite the Marian Rosary in a church or public oratory or in a family group, a religious community, or pious association.
3. Read Sacred Scripture with due veneration for at least one half hour.
4. Piously make the Way of the Cross.

There are a good number of other works that qualify for a plenary indulgence on certain days or occasions.[205] What if a person tries to gain a plenary indulgence but is not adequately detached from venial sin? He would gain a powerful partial indulgence.

## Partial Indulgences

A partial indulgence is one that removes part of a person's temporal punishment — part of one's purgatorial debt. There are many works or activities for which you can gain a partial indulgence. I list just a few of them here:

1. Devoutly use an article of devotion (a crucifix or cross, a rosary, a scapular, or a medal) blessed by a priest.

---

[205] See http://www.mycatholicsource.com/mcs/cg/indulgences.htm for a list.

2. Teach or study Christian doctrine.

3. Participate in a public novena before the feasts of Christmas, Pentecost, or the Immaculate Conception.

4. Recite a prayer approved by the Church for priestly or religious vocations.[206]

5. Spend some time in mental prayer.

6. Listen with devotion to a homily.

7. Read Sacred Scripture with due veneration.

8. Make the Sign of the Cross devotedly, while saying, "In the name of the Father and of the Son and of the Holy Spirit" (at least inwardly).

9. Visit the Blessed Sacrament for any period of time.

10. Pray the Rosary privately.

"Participation in the Sacrifice of the Mass or the Sacraments is not enriched by indulgences due to the surpassing [power] … that they have in themselves."[207]

### General Activities

There are three other "general grants" for gaining a partial indulgence:

1. While performing your duties and in dealing with hardships, raise your mind in humble confidence to God, adding — even if only mentally — some pious words. (An example of the latter might be to say "Praise God" in a difficult situation.)

---

[206] See, for example, Prayer for Vocations, United States Conference of Catholic Bishops, https://www.usccb.org/resources/prayer-vocations.

[207] *Enchiridion*, "Preliminary Observations," no. 3.

2. In a spirit of faith and mercy, give of yourself or your goods to serve brothers or sisters in need.
3. In a spirit of penance, deprive yourself of what is licit and pleasing (e.g., fast).

The souls in purgatory are in desperate need of our prayers and indulgences. I offer any indulgence I might receive for the souls in purgatory but have asked the Blessed Mother to arrange that my last plenary indulgence be for myself. What a blessing it would be to meet perhaps hundreds or thousands of souls in heaven and receive their thankful embrace for lessening their time in purgatory.

It is in our best interest to be aware of indulgences and to ask that we might receive them for whatever religious acts we participate in. Then we should try to seldom think about them, lest we obsess over them.

# About the Author

Father T. G. Morrow worked for twelve years as an engineer before entering the seminary and being ordained a priest for the Archdiocese of Washington in 1982. He was host for three years (1989–1992) of *Catholic Faith Alive!*, a radio program on which he explained the Catholic Faith. He is cofounder of the St. Catherine Society and St. Lawrence Society for single women and men, respectively, which are still active in the Washington, DC, area. Fr. Morrow has an S.T.L. in moral theology from the Dominican House of Studies and a doctorate in sacred theology from the Pope John Paul II Institute for Studies on Marriage and Family.

His book *Christian Dating in A Godless World* (formerly, *Christian Courtship in An Oversexed World*) is now in its fourth printing, published by Sophia Institute Press (now available in Spanish and Portuguese). His other published works include *Be Holy*; *Achieving Chastity in a Pornographic World*; *Who's Who in Heaven*; *Overcoming Sinful Anger*; *Fatima in Brief*; and *Amazing Saints*. All of his writing can be seen at www.cfalive.com.

Thank you for reading this book. If you would like to contact the author to comment on the book or to request a speaking engagement by Fr. Morrow, kindly contact him at morrowt@adw.org.

# Sophia Institute

Sophia Institute is a nonprofit institution that seeks to nurture the spiritual, moral, and cultural life of souls and to spread the Gospel of Christ in conformity with the authentic teachings of the Roman Catholic Church.

Sophia Institute Press fulfills this mission by offering translations, reprints, and new publications that afford readers a rich source of the enduring wisdom of mankind.

Sophia Institute also operates the popular online resource CatholicExchange.com. *Catholic Exchange* provides world news from a Catholic perspective as well as daily devotionals and articles that will help readers to grow in holiness and live a life consistent with the teachings of the Church.

In 2013, Sophia Institute launched Sophia Institute for Teachers to renew and rebuild Catholic culture through service to Catholic education. With the goal of nurturing the spiritual, moral, and cultural life of souls, and an abiding respect for the role and work of teachers, we strive to provide materials and programs that are at once enlightening to the mind and ennobling to the heart; faithful and complete, as well as useful and practical.

Sophia Institute gratefully recognizes the Solidarity Association for preserving and encouraging the growth of our apostolate over the course of many years. Without their generous and timely support, this book would not be in your hands.

www.SophiaInstitute.com
www.CatholicExchange.com
www.SophiaInstituteforTeachers.org

Sophia Institute Press® is a registered trademark of Sophia Institute. Sophia Institute is a tax-exempt institution as defined by the Internal Revenue Code, Section 501(c)(3). Tax ID 22-2548708.